E1/E2

Maths
The Basic Skills

Number

Veronica Thomas

Series contributors
June Haighton
Deborah Holder

Nelson Thornes
a Wolters Kluwer business

Text © J Haighton, D Holder, V Thomas, 2006
Original illustrations © Nelson Thornes Ltd 2006

Published in 2006 by:
Nelson Thornes Ltd
Delta Place
27 Bath Road
CHELTENHAM
GL53 7TH
United Kingdom

06 07 08 09/10 9 8 7 6 5 4 3 2 1

A catalogue record for this book is available from the British Library

ISBN 0 7487 8331 8

Illustrations by Tech-Set Ltd, Gateshead, Tyne & Wear
Page make-up by Tech-Set Ltd, Gateshead, Tyne & Wear

Printed in Croatia by Zrinski

Contents

Numbers

Calculations

Add and subtract

Multiply

Rounding

Using the signs + − × and using a calculator

Calculations skill check

Fractions

Fractions skill check

Number mock tests

Answers

Count to 10 and back

Write the next number.

1 1 2 3 4 5 ___

2 3 4 5 6 ___

3 7 8 9 ___

4 10 9 8 7 ___

5 5 4 3 2 ___

6 8 7 6 5 ___

Write in the missing numbers.

7 1 ___ 3 ___ 5 6 ___ 8 ___ 10

8 10 9 ___ 7 6 5 ___ 3 ___ 1

How many tins?

0	1	2	3	4	5	6	7	8	9	10
zero	one	two	three	four	five	six	seven	eight	nine	ten

1   four 4

2

3

4

5

6

7

8

9

10

1	2	3	4	5	6	7	8	9	10
one	two	three	four	five	six	seven	eight	nine	ten

How many towels are on each washing line?

Example

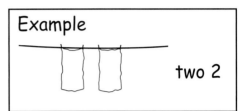

two 2

1  _____ _____

2 _____ _____

3  _____ _____

4  _____ _____

5  _____ _____

6 _____ _____

How many towels are in each basket?

7 _____ _____   **8** _____ _____

9 _____ _____   **10** _____ _____

Numbers in words and figures

1	2	3	4	5	6	7	8	9	10
one	two	three	four	five	six	seven	eight	nine	ten

1 Put the players' numbers on their shirts.

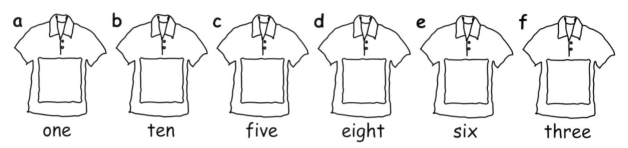

one   ten   five   eight   six   three

2 Write the numbers on the cards in words.

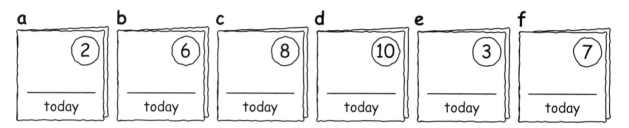

a (2) today   b (6) today   c (8) today   d (10) today   e (3) today   f (7) today

3 Put the numbers on the cards.

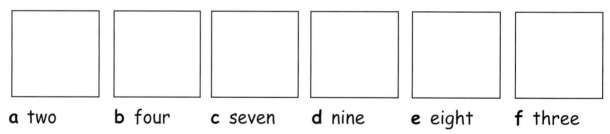

a two   **b** four   **c** seven   **d** nine   **e** eight   **f** three

4 Write the amount in words on each cheque.

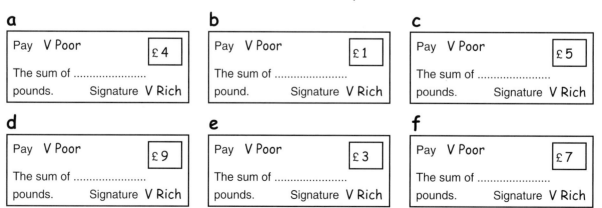

a
Pay V Poor   £ 4
The sum of ....
pounds.   Signature V Rich

b
Pay V Poor   £ 1
The sum of ....
pound.   Signature V Rich

c
Pay V Poor   £ 5
The sum of ....
pounds.   Signature V Rich

d
Pay V Poor   £ 9
The sum of ....
pounds.   Signature V Rich

e
Pay V Poor   £ 3
The sum of ....
pounds.   Signature V Rich

f
Pay V Poor   £ 7
The sum of ....
pounds.   Signature V Rich

Which floor?

Shade the button each person should press.

1	2
3	4
5	6
7	8
9	10

1 Mr Hussain
2nd floor

1	2
3	4
5	6
7	8
9	10

2 Mr Jackson
6th floor

1	2
3	4
5	6
7	8
9	10

3 Mrs Jones
4th floor

1	2
3	4
5	6
7	8
9	10

4 Mr McDonald
3rd floor

1	2
3	4
5	6
7	8
9	10

5 Mrs Griffith
8th floor

1	2
3	4
5	6
7	8
9	10

6 Mr Minogue
9th floor

1	2
3	4
5	6
7	8
9	10

7 Mr Panesar
5th floor

1	2
3	4
5	6
7	8
9	10

8 Mr Poliniski
1st floor

1	2
3	4
5	6
7	8
9	10

9 Mrs Wing
10th floor

Tim Ben Jo Jill Max Deb Raj Sona Pete

1 Who is first in the line? _____

2 Who is last in the line? _____

3 Who is second in the line? _____

4 Who is third in the line? _____

5 Who is 7th in the line? _____

6 Who is 4th in the line? _____

7 Who is 9th in the line? _____

8 Who is 5th in the line? _____

9 Where is Deb in the line? _____

10 Where is Max in the line? _____

11 Where is Sona in the line? _____

12 Where is Jo in the line? _____

More or less?

Example			Pat has three tomatoes. Bill has four tomatoes. Bill has **more** than Pat. Pat has **less** than Bill.
		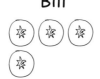	

Write in the missing words:

more	less

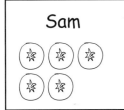 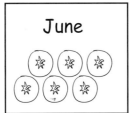

1 a Sam has _____ than June.

b June has _____ than Sam.

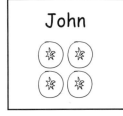 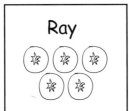

2 a Ray has _____ than John.

b John has _____ than Ray.

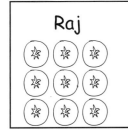 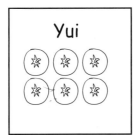

3 a Raj has _____ than Yui.

b Yui has _____ than Raj.

 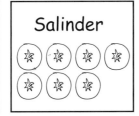

4 a Salinder has _____ than Pete.

b Pete has _____ than Salinder.

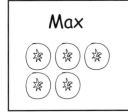 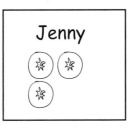

5 a Max has _____ than Jenny.

b Jenny has _____ than Max.

How many:

1 **a** books?

     b books?

2 **a** apples?

     b apples?

3 **a** pencils?

     b pencils?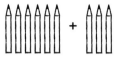

4 **a** cakes?

     b cakes?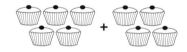

5 **a** pencil sharpeners?

     b pencil sharpeners?

6 **a** calculators?

     b calculators?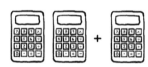

7 **a** buttons?

     b buttons?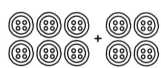

8 **a** pens?

     b pens?

9 **a** batteries?

     b batteries?

10 **a** rulers?

     b rulers?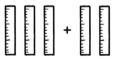

11 **a** flowers?

     b flowers?

Count to 20

How many cakes are on each shelf?

1  .... cakes

2 .... cakes

3 .... cakes

4 .... cakes

5 .... cakes

6 .... cakes

How many cakes are in each box?

7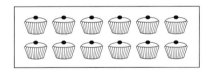

.... cakes

8

.... cakes

9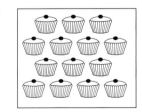

.... cakes

10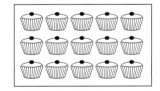

.... cakes

Count in 2s

1 Fill in the missing numbers.

1 __ 3 __ 5 __ 7 __ 9 __ 11 __ 13 __ 15 __ 17 __ 19 20

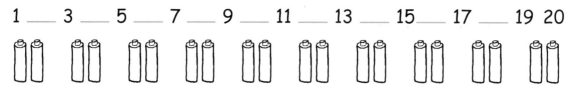

How many batteries? Count them in 2s.

2

Answer _____

3

Answer _____

4

Answer _____

How many nails? Count these in 2s.

5

Answer _____

6

Answer _____

7

Answer _____

Numbers

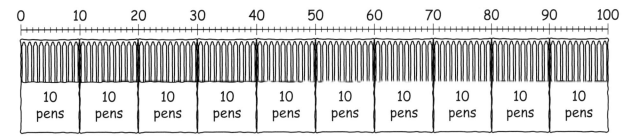

How many pens? Count the full packets in 10s.

1 Answer _____

2 Answer _____

3 Answer _____

4 Answer _____

5 Answer _____

Count on in 10s

Remember
Only the **Tens** column changes when you count on (add 10).
Count on 10 from 13.

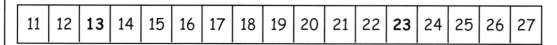

| 11 | 12 | **13** | 14 | 15 | 16 | 17 | 18 | 19 | 20 | 21 | 22 | **23** | 24 | 25 | 26 | 27 |

TU
13 has 1 **Ten** and 3 **Units**

TU
23 has 2 **Tens** and 3 **Units**

1 Add 10 to each of the following numbers.

  a 8 _____

  b 12 _____

  c 9 _____

  d 16 _____

  e 22 _____

  f 31 _____

  g 24 _____

  h 36 _____

  i 14 _____

  j 45 _____

  k 53 _____

  l 27 _____

2 How old will each person be in ten years time?

  a Tom _____
     age 6

  b Bill _____
     age 13

  c Eli _____
     age 7

  d Reg _____
     age 15

  e Satvinder _____
     age 42

  f Josh _____
     age 57

  g Mia _____
     age 71

  h Cara _____
     age 65

3 Add 10p to the cost of each item.

  a 32p _____

  b 44p _____

  c 58p _____

  d 72p _____

  e 66p _____

  f 48p _____

  g 61p _____

  h 14p _____

Tens and units

Remember		T	U
forty-one	has 4 Tens and 1 Unit	4	1

Write these numbers in Tens and Units.

						T	U
1	thirty-six	has ____ Tens and ____ Units				____	____
2	twenty-seven	has ____ Tens and ____ Units				____	____
3	sixty-one	has ____ Tens and ____ Unit				____	____
4	seventy-three	has ____ Tens and ____ Units				____	____
5	forty	has ____ Tens and ____ Units				____	____
6	forty-eight	has ____ Tens and ____ Units				____	____
7	fifty	has ____ Tens and ____ Units				____	____
8	thirteen	has ____ Ten and ____ Units				____	____
9	seven	has ____ Tens and ____ Units				____	____
10	eighty	has ____ Tens and ____ Units				____	____
11	three	has ____ Tens and ____ Units				____	____
12	sixteen	has ____ Ten and ____ Units				____	____

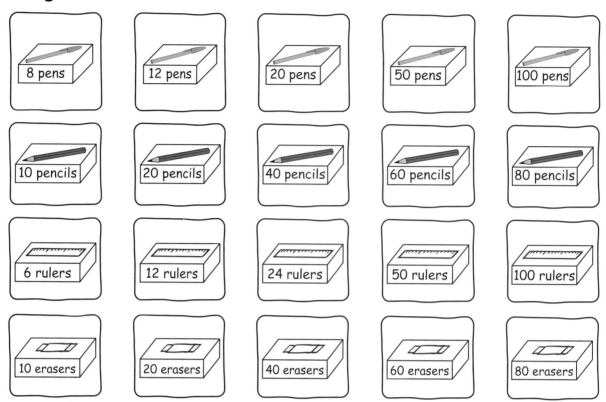

There are different tests going on at college.

Choose one pack the right size so each person has at least one pen, pencil, ruler and eraser with as few as possible left over.

1 (8 people are having a test.)

pens _____ pencils _____

rulers _____ erasers _____

2 (18 people are having a test.)

pens _____ pencils _____

rulers _____ erasers _____

3 (32 people are having a test.)

pens _____ pencils _____

rulers _____ erasers _____

4 (48 people are having a test.)

pens _____ pencils _____

rulers _____ erasers _____

5 (72 people are having a test.)

pens _____ pencils _____

rulers _____ erasers _____

Odd and even numbers

> **Remember**
>
> Even numbers can be divided into 2s exactly
>
> 6 is an even number
>
> Odd numbers cannot be divided into 2s exactly
>
> 7 is an odd number
>
> Even numbers end in **2 4 6 8** or **0**
>
> | 2 | 4 | 6 | 8 | 10 |
> |----|----|----|----|----|
> | 12 | 14 | 16 | 18 | 20 |
> | 22 | 24 | 26 | 28 | 30 |

1 Which of these are even numbers? Circle the even numbers.

   3   6   9   14   19   20   26   29   32   35   42

2 Write down 5 more even numbers. _____ _____ _____ _____ _____

3 Which of these are odd numbers? Circle the odd numbers.

   4   7   8   11   16   19   22   27   28   31   34

4 Write down 5 more odd numbers. _____ _____ _____ _____ _____

5 The house numbers on one side of a street are all even and on the other side are all odd.
Draw a line to show which side each letter is for.
The first one has been done for you.

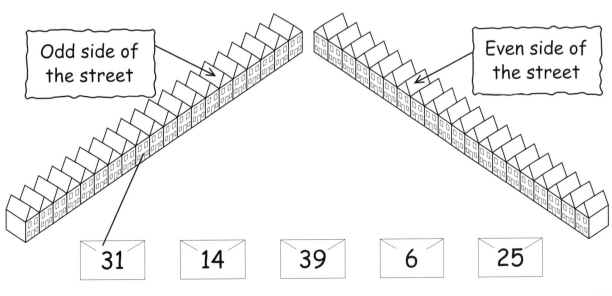

Odd one out

Some clothes are packed in 2s to make a pair.
Will there be an odd one out? Answer yes or no.

Remember Even numbers can be divided in 2s exactly.

Odd one out?

1

2 socks make
a pair

Number of socks

a 9 socks   _____

b 8 socks   _____

c 7 socks   _____

2

2 shoes make
a pair

Number of shoes

a 7 shoes   _____

b 14 shoes   _____

c 17 shoes   _____

3

2 gloves make
a pair

Number of gloves

a 13 gloves   _____

b 18 gloves   _____

c 20 gloves   _____

4

2 shin pads make
a pair

Number of shin pads

a 19 shin pads   _____

b 26 shin pads   _____

c 27 shin pads   _____

1 How many cans are there? _____

2 How many mugs are there? _____

p7-8

3 Are there more cans than mugs? _____

p4-6

4 a The number of boxes is written down.
Fill in the missing words and numbers.
The first one has been done for you.

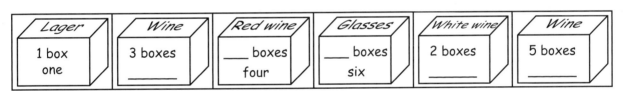

Lager	Wine	Red wine	Glasses	White wine	Wine
1 box one	3 boxes ____	____ boxes four	____ boxes six	2 boxes ____	5 boxes ____

  b Write the numbers in order   **1** ___ ___ ___ ___ ___

5 These are prizes.

1st first	____ fourth	____ sixth	____ third	____ fifth	____ seventh	____ second

  a Write in the missing numbers. The first one has been done for you.

  b Write the numbers in order.

  1st ___ ___ ___ ___ ___ ___

  first ___ ___ ___ ___ ___ ___

p9

1 Fill in the missing numbers.

1   2   3 __ 5 __ 7 __ 9 __ __ __

13 __ 15 __ 17 __ 19 __ 21 __ 23 __

p11-13

2 In a final test each student gains 10 marks.
Add 10 to each student's test results.

Test results					
Jen	39 ____	Deb	42 ____	Mick	21 ____
Alice	76 ____	Karl	28 ____	Sian	36 ____
Ben	55 ____	Ray	24 ____	Stan	43 ____
Andy	17 ____	Sonia	63 ____	Rajaa	88 ____

3 Each student and the tutor take a partner to a party.
There are 11 students and one tutor.
How many people go to the party?

_____

4 Deb has

She finds 20p in the road. How much has she now?

_____

p15-16

5 Deb finds a letter in the road.

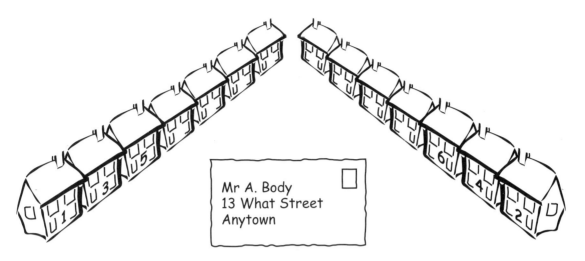

Mr A. Body
13 What Street
Anytown

Left side   Right side

On which side of the street is number 13?

_____

p13-14

6

| 0 | 5 | 2 |

a What is the largest 2 digit number you can make from these numbers?

_____

b What is the smallest 2 digit number you can make from these numbers?

_____

Numbers skill check 1 answers

1   6

2   4

3   Yes

4   a

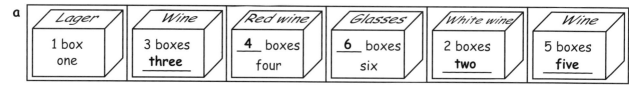

   b   1 2 3 4 5 6

5   a

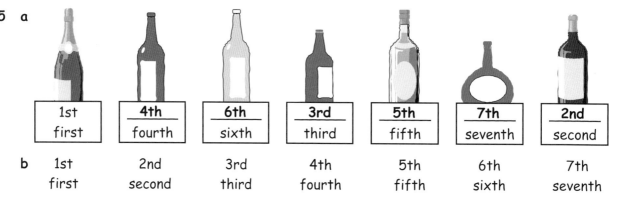

| 1st first | 4th fourth | 6th sixth | 3rd third | 5th fifth | 7th seventh | 2nd second |

   b

| 1st first | 2nd second | 3rd third | 4th fourth | 5th fifth | 6th sixth | 7th seventh |

Numbers skill check 2 answers

1   1 2 3 **4** 5 **6** 7 **8** 9 **10 11** 12 13 **14** 15 **16** 17 **18** 19 **20** 21 **22** 23 **24**

2

Jen	49	Deb	52	Mick	31	Alice	86
Karl	38	Sian	46	Ben	65	Ray	34
Stan	53	Andy	27	Sonia	73	Rajaa	98

3   24

4   70p

5   left side

6   a   52

    b   20

Add up the bottles

Example
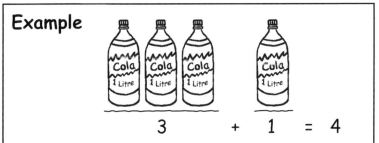
3   +   1   =   4

1

2   +   5 = _____

3

4   +   5 = _____

5

6   + 3 = _____

7

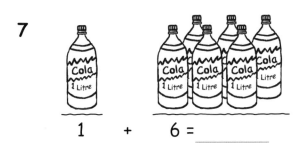

1   +   6 = _____

9

4   + 4 = _____

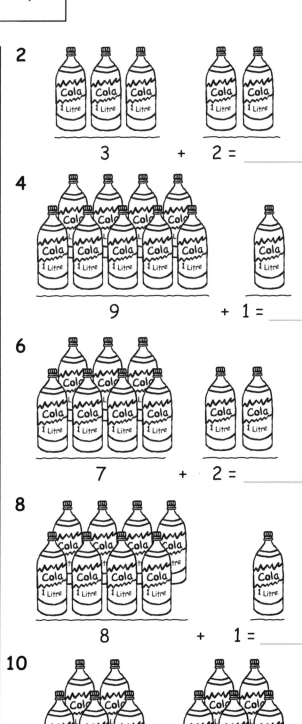

2

3   +   2 = _____

4

9   + 1 = _____

6

7   +   2 = _____

8

8   +   1 = _____

10

5   +   5 = _____

Make ten

How many bottles need to be added to make 10?

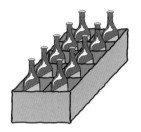

1 　　　　　　　+ _____ = 10

2 　　　　　　　+ _____ = 10

3 　　　　　　　+ _____ = 10

4 　　　　　　　+ _____ = 10

5 　　　　　　　+ _____ = 10

6 　　　　　　　+ _____ = 10

7 　　　　　　　+ _____ = 10

8 　　　　　　　+ _____ = 10

9 　　　　　　　+ _____ = 10

Calculations

Make ten again

1 Match the numbers to make 10.
The first has been done for you.

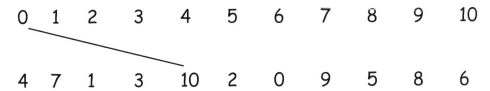

0   1   2   3   4   5   6   7   8   9   10

4   7   1   3   10   2   0   9   5   8   6

2 How many pencils need to be added to each group to make ten?

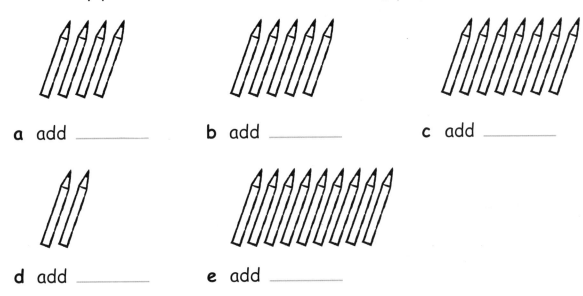

a add _____

b add _____

c add _____

d add _____

e add _____

3 Match the numbers to make ten. The first one has been done for you.

one   nine   three

eight   five   four

two   six   zero

five   ten   seven

How many more?

How many more:

1 triangles △ are there than squares ☐ ? _____

2 triangles △ are there than rectangles ▯ ? _____

3 stars ☆ are there than arrows ⇨ ? _____

4 rectangles ▯ are there than arrows ⇨ ? _____

5 squares ☐ are there than rectangles ▯ ? _____

6 stars ☆ are there than squares ☐ ? _____

7 circles ◯ are there than rectangles ▯ ? _____

Make connections

Fill in the missing numbers.

1 a If $8 - 2 = 6$ then $6 + \boxed{} = 8$

8	–	2	=	
		ı		ı
	–		=	2
=		=		=
2	+		=	8

b If $6 - 4 = 2$ then $2 + \boxed{} = 6$

2 a If $7 - 4 = 3$ then $4 + \boxed{} = 7$

7	–		=	3
–		–		+
	+		=	4
=		=		=
4	+		=	

b If $4 - 1 = 3$ then $3 + \boxed{} = 4$

3 a If $9 - 7 = 2$ then $2 + \boxed{} = 9$

9	–	7	=	
–		–		+
	+		=	
=		=		=
7	+		=	9

b If $7 - 5 = 2$ then $2 + \boxed{} = 7$

4 a If $8 - 3 = 5$ then $5 + \boxed{} = 8$

	–	3	=	5
–		–		+
3	+		=	3
=		=		=
5	+	3	=	

b If $3 - 0 = 3$ then $0 + \boxed{} = 3$

5 a If $10 - 4 = 6$ then $6 + \boxed{} = 10$

10	–		=	6
–		+		+
6	–	2	=	
=		=		=
	+		=	10

b If $6 - 2 = 4$ then $2 + \boxed{} = 6$

magazine
£2

chocolates
£6

CD
£9

phone card
£10

pen
£3

newspaper
£1

bus pass
£8

camera
£7

batteries
£5

wine
£4

1 How much is it for the

   a wine and newspaper? _____

   b chocolates and magazine? _____

   c CD and newspaper? _____

   d camera and pen? _____

2 How much more

   a is the phone card than the bus pass? _____

   b are the chocolates than the wine? _____

   c is the camera than the batteries? _____

   d is the CD than the magazine? _____

3 How much change should you get from £10 for each item?

   a magazine   **b** chocolates   **c** CD   **d** phone card **e** pen

   £ _____   £ _____   £ _____   £ _____   £ _____

   f newspaper **g** bus pass   **h** camera   **i** batteries   **j** wine

   £ _____   £ _____   £ _____   £ _____   £ _____

College classes

Each person has a different number of classes at college.

These people want **more** classes.
How many classes do they want?

> **Example**
> Suzy has 5 classes.
> She wants 2 **more**.
> 5 + 2 = 7 classes

1 Jim has 6 classes.

He wants 2 more.

_____ classes

2 Farhya has 3 classes.

She wants 3 more.

_____ classes

3 Pete has 5 classes.

He wants 3 more.

_____ classes

4 Sandra has 4 classes.

She wants 2 more.

_____ classes

5 Bilal has 4 classes.

He wants 2 more.

_____ classes

6 Carla has 7 classes.

She wants 3 more.

_____ classes

These people want **less** classes.
How many classes do they want?

> **Example**
> Pat has 5 classes.
> She wants 2 **less**.
> 5 − 2 = 3 classes

7 Kim has 3 classes.

She wants 2 less.

_____ class

8 Frida has 5 classes.

She wants 3 less.

_____ classes

9 Raj has 7 classes.

He wants 3 less.

_____ classes

10 Steve has 4 classes.

He wants 2 less.

_____ classes

11 Jo has 6 classes.

He wants 4 less.

_____ classes

12 Cath has 6 classes.

She wants 3 less.

_____ classes

Add up in your head

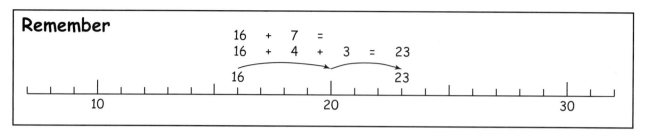

Remember

16 + 7 =
16 + 4 + 3 = 23

16   23

1 17 + 6 = _____

2 28 + 9 = _____

3 32 + 9 = _____

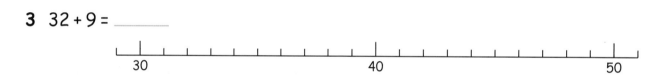

4 46 + 8 = _____

5 55 + 6 = _____

6 68 + 8 = _____

7 74 + 7 = _____

8 85 + 9 = _____

Calculations

Remember

```
T U
4 1 +
2 6
───
6 7
```

Add the Units: 1 + 6 = 7

Then add the Tens: 4 + 2 = 6

and

```
T U
3 6 +
2 7
───
6 3  ←───── Put the 3 in the Units.
  1  ←───── Put the Ten with the other Tens. (You can put this at the top if
                                                you prefer.)
```

Add the Units: 6 + 7 = 13

13 has 1 Ten and 3 Units

Add the Tens: 3 + 2 + 1 = 6

1	2	3	4	5	6
2 4 +	4 2 +	3 6 +	2 3 +	4 0 +	3 8 +
3 4	2 7	6 3	5 5	3 7	5 0

7	8	9	10	11	12
4 3 +	6 3 +	2 6 +	4 6 +	2 8 +	5 3 +
3 8	1 8	3 8	3 4	4 7	3 9

13	14	15	16	17	18
2 6 +	4 0 +	5 4 +	2 9 +	3 9 +	4 0 +
5 7	3 0	3 4	3 5	5 2	2 8

19	20	21	22	23	24
4 8 +	3 6 +	5 4 +	2 2 +	3 1 +	2 8 +
3 2	4 6	1 6	4 5	5 6	2 8

Example	23 + 28 =

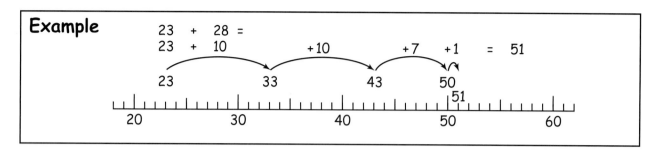

1 26 + 25 = _____

2 36 + 22 = _____

3 39 + 18 = _____

4 33 + 26 = _____

5 44 + 28 = _____

6 47 + 34 = _____

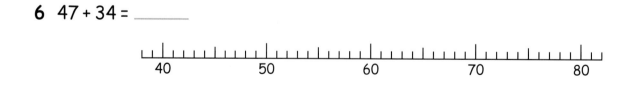

7 52 + 19 = _____

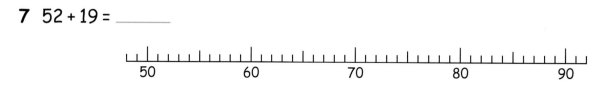

Other ways to add up in your head

> **Remember**
>
> **Method 1** 38 + 17
>
> 38 is nearly 40:   40 + 17 = 57   (easier to do in your head)
> 40 is 2 more than 38:   57 - 2 = 55   (so take off 2)
>
> **Method 2** 42 + 17
>
> Break 42 into 40 and 2.
> Add all the numbers together in an order
> that is easier to do in your head: 40 + 17 = 57 + 2 = 59

Do these in your head. Use any method you like.

1 37 + 36 = _____   **2** 28 + 27 = _____   **3** 37 + 48 = _____

4 29 + 34 = _____   **5** 26 + 54 = _____   **6** 43 + 48 = _____

7 17 + 54 = _____   **8** 32 + 49 = _____   **9** 45 + 45 = _____

10 26 + 37 = _____   **11** 63 + 28 = _____   **12** 33 + 49 = _____

13 72 + 19 = _____   **14** 66 + 24 = _____   **15** 34 + 39 = _____

16 43 + 29 = _____   **17** 28 + 51 = _____   **18** 42 + 38 = _____

Addition problems

1 Jill is 43. Bill is 8 years older than Jill.
How old is Bill?

Answer _____

2 There are 26 people on a train. 8 more people get on.
How many people are on the train now?

Answer _____

3 Ben has 18 cards. He finds 6 more.
How many cards has he now?

Answer _____

4 Mohammed pays £47 pounds for a mobile phone and
£8 for a phone case. How much is this altogether?

Answer _____

5 There are 24 cars in the car park. 7 more cars go into
the car park. How many cars are in the car park now?

Answer _____

6 Jan is 32. In 6 years time she hopes to be self-employed.
How old will she be then?

Answer _____

7 The 1st rugby match is on 15th September.
The 2nd match is one week later.
What is the date of the 2nd match?

Answer _____

8 Jess buys a bag for £26 and a hat for £7.
How much is this in total?

Answer _____

9 The weekly shop costs £48. It goes up £5.
What is the weekly cost now?

Answer _____

10 28 people are invited to a party. 7 more people turn up.
How many people are at the party?

Answer _____

joystick £29

computer game £28

DVD £18

single CD £14

blank video £8

head phones £14

double CD £28

game boy game £15

DVD player £38

DVD storage £35

CD rack £22

CD box set £39

play station £55

personal CD player £47

camera £49

game boy case £12

A shop is giving £60 worth of goods free to prize winners.

List as many sets of prizes as you can.
Add the prices in your head.

Matches

Find the total number of matches held each month at the 2 leisure centres. Add the numbers in your head. Check each answer by writing the numbers in columns and adding them.

	Month	Number of matches		Total number of matches
		Stockton	Boldmere	
1	January	17	24	
2	February	28	31	
3	March	27	36	
4	April	45	48	
5	May	36	48	
6	June	33	63	
7	July	39	52	
8	August	29	24	
9	September	33	28	
10	October	38	47	
11	November	29	35	
12	December	18	27	

Calculations

Make connections again

Fill in the missing numbers.

1 a If 16 – 3 = 13   then   13 + ☐ = 16

b If 3 – 0 = 3   then   3 + ☐ = 3

16	–	3	=	
–		+		+
	–		=	3
=		=		=
13	+		=	

2 a If 19 – 15 = 4   then   4 + ☐ = 19

b If 15 – 11 = 4   then   4 + ☐ = 15

19	–		=	4
–		–		+
	+		=	15
=		=		=
15	+		=	

3 a If 17 – 12 = 5   then   5 + ☐ = 17

b If 12 – 7 = 5   then   5 + ☐ = 12

17	–	12	=	
–		–		+
	+		=	
=		=		=
12	+		=	17

4 a If 15 – 7 = 8   then   7 + ☐ = 15

b If 8 – 1 = 7   then   7 + ☐ = 8

	–	8	=	7
–		–		+
7	+		=	8
=		=		=
8	+	7	=	

5 a If 18 – 6 = 12   then   12 + ☐ = 18

b If 6 – 0 = 6   then   6 + ☐ = 6

18	–		=	12
–		–		+
6	+		=	
=		=		=
	+		=	18

Example 39 - 24

Count on from the smaller number to the nearest multiple of 10

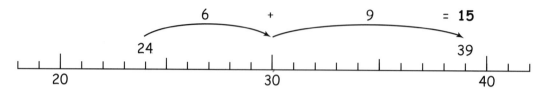

so 39 – 24 = 15

1 25 – 16 = _____

2 28 – 17 = _____

3 35 – 22 = _____

4 53 – 44 = _____

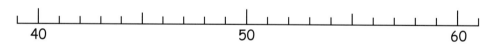

5 67 – 52 = _____

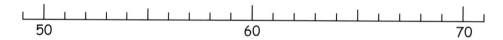

6 73 – 66 = _____

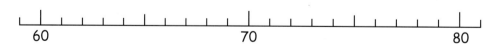

7 87 – 78 = _____

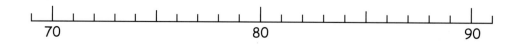

Remember

Method 1

36 – 21

21 is nearly 20:   36 – 20 = 16   (easier to do in your head)
20 is 1 less than 21:   16 – 1 = 15   (so take another 1)

Method 2

42 - 16

Count on from the smaller number to the nearest multiple of 10.
Then count on in 10s:

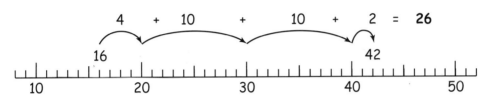

Do these in your head. Use any method you like.

1 40 – 16 = _____   **2** 34 – 17 = _____   **3** 45 – 18 _____

4 43 – 23 = _____   **5** 46 – 16 = _____   **6** 42 – 22 = _____

7 54 – 27 = _____   **8** 71 – 44 = _____   **9** 72 – 36 = _____

10 54 – 23 = _____   **11** 66 – 28 = _____   **12** 91 – 44 = _____

13 89 – 50 = _____   **14** 42 – 17 = _____   **15** 98 – 39 = _____

16 68 – 31 = _____   **17** 81 – 52 = _____   **18** 100 – 36 = _____

Remember

T	U
4	5	−
2	4
2	1

4 5 −   Start with the Units. 5 − 4 = 1
2 4   Then subtract the Tens. 4 − 2 = 2
2 1

If you need to borrow:

T U   Start with the Units.
⁶7̸ ¹2 −   You cannot subtract 9 from 2, so borrow a Ten. This leaves 6 Tens
  4 9   Put the Ten with the 2 Units to make 12. 12 − 9 = 3
  2 3   There are 6 Tens left. 6 − 4 = 2

Or use the payback method:

T U   Start with the Units.
7 ¹2 −   You cannot subtract 9 from 2, so add a Ten and put it with the
⁵4̸ 9   2 Units to make 12. 12 − 9 = 3
  2 3   Then pay a Ten back to the number in the Tens column that
         you are subtracting. The number 4 becomes a 5. 7 − 5 = 2

No borrowing

1 3 7 −   **2** 4 6 −   **3** 4 9 −   **4** 5 8 −   **5** 7 3 −   **6** 6 6 −
     1 7   3 0   3 2   1 7   2 1   3 4
   ‾‾‾‾   ‾‾‾‾   ‾‾‾‾   ‾‾‾‾   ‾‾‾‾   ‾‾‾‾

With borrowing

7 6 0 −   **8** 7 2 −   **9** 4 0 −   **10** 6 2 −   **11** 7 3 −   **12** 9 0 −
     4 7   2 7   2 3   1 8   3 7   1 9
   ‾‾‾‾   ‾‾‾‾   ‾‾‾‾   ‾‾‾‾   ‾‾‾‾   ‾‾‾‾

Subtraction practice

1 78 −	2 46 −	3 49 −	4 64 −	5 77 −	6 90 −
22	23	17	36	48	16
————	————	————	————	————	————

7 99 −	8 80 −	9 70 −	10 54 −	11 23 −	12 36 −
71	32	34	19	18	18
————	————	————	————	————	————

How much will each person have left after buying each item?

Item and price	Ellie has £55	Jake has £72	Yusuf has £80	Rajaa has £96
Mobile phone £44				
Art set £23				
Watch £29				
Suitcase set £32				
Head phones £17				
Coat £43				

Subtraction problems

1 A shop has 32 TVs. 9 are sold. How many are left?

Answer _____

2 Today is 27th September.
   How many days ago was 15th September?

Answer _____

3 Max has £53. He spends £27.
   How much does he have left?

Answer _____

4 32 people enrol on a class.
   The day changes and 17 people can no longer go to the class.
   How many people are left in the class?

Answer _____

5 There are 42 dog treats in a bag. The dogs eat 7.
   How many are left?

Answer _____

6 There are 50 tickets for a concert. 39 are sold.
   How many are left?

Answer _____

7 A DVD player is reduced from £57 to £43.
   How much is saved?

Answer _____

8 A doctor had 95 patients on his books last year.
   This year he has 86.
   How many more patients were there last year?

Answer _____

9 There are 56 tins in a stack.
   Some fall off and 48 tins are left.
   How many tins fell off?

Answer _____

10 A football match lasts 90 minutes.
   The match started 25 minutes ago.
   How much time is left?

Answer _____

Calculations

Attendance

The table below shows students' attendance in classes.

The number on the top is the number of times they ⟶ 56
attended classes.

The number on the bottom is the total number of classes. ⟶ 70

Find how many classes each student missed.
Use a mental or a written method. Check your answer by adding the number of classes missed to the number of classes attended.
The total should be 70.

	student	attendance	number of classes missed
1	B. Singh	$\frac{56}{70}$	
2	T. Jones	$\frac{63}{70}$	
3	L. Smith	$\frac{34}{70}$	
4	C. Kaur	$\frac{49}{70}$	
5	D. Hussain	$\frac{51}{70}$	
6	P. Long	$\frac{62}{70}$	
7	E. Turner	$\frac{59}{70}$	
8	S. Harris	$\frac{41}{70}$	
9	G. Bowman	$\frac{39}{70}$	

Multiplication

Example How many cans?

4   +   4   +   4   +   4   = 4 x 4 = 16

How many

1   pens?

5 + 5 + 5 + 5 + 5 + 5 = _____

2   £?

2 + 2 + 2 + 2 + 2 = _____

3   batteries?

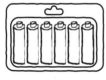 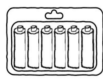 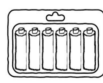 

6   +   6   +   6   +   6   = _____

4   sausages?

8   +   8   +   8   +   8   +   8   = _____

5   videos?

3 + 3 + 3 + 3 + 3 + 3 = _____

           Calculations

Remember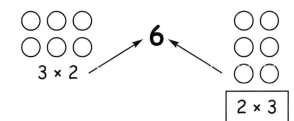

3 x 2 and 2 x 3 gives the same answer

1 ○○○○   **32**
○○○○

a ○○○○
○○○○
○○○○
○○○○
○○○○
○○○○
○○○○

2 ○○○○○○○○   **8**
○○○○○○○○
○○○○○○○○
○○○○○○○○

b ○○○○○○
○○○○○○
○○○○○○

3 ○○○   **18**
○○○
○○○
○○○
○○○
○○○

c ○○
○○
○○
○○

Answer each sum.
Draw a line to match the sums. The first has been done for you.

4 3 x 7 = 21   **d** 3 x 9

5 8 x 2 = ___   **e** 7 x 3

6 9 x 3 = ___   **f** 5 x 4

7 6 x 7 = ___   **g** 2 x 8

8 4 x 5 = ___   **h** 7 x 4

9 4 x 7 = ___   **i** 7 x 6

Another odd one out

3 sums in each set have the same answer.
Circle the sum which has a different answer.

1	4 x 3	2	9 x 2	3	4 x 4
	2 x 6		1 x 18		2 x 8
	1 x 12		2 x 8		1 x 16
	3 x 3		2 x 9		7 x 3

4	4 x 8	5	15 x 1	6	2 x 5
	3 x 8		3 x 5		1 x 10
	24 x 1		6 x 2		3 x 3
	4 x 6		5 x 3		5 x 2

7	7 x 3	8	6 x 5	9	9 x 4
	4 x 5		4 x 7		6 x 6
	2 x 10		3 x 10		5 x 7
	20 x 1		5 x 6		4 x 9

Calculations

Table sequences

Continue each sequence.

2s   2   4   6   ___ ___ ___ ___ ___

3s   3   6   9   ___ ___ ___ ___ ___

4s   4   8   12   ___ ___ ___ ___ ___

5s   5   10   15   ___ ___ ___ ___ ___

6s   6   12   18   ___ ___ ___ ___ ___

7s   7   14   21   ___ ___ ___ ___ ___

8s   8   16   24   ___ ___ ___ ___ ___

9s   9   18   27   ___ ___ ___ ___ ___

10s   10   20   30   ___ ___ ___ ___ ___

Mini darts

Practise the 2 times table and 3 times table.

Double the score in the outside ring. (x 2)

Triple the score in the inside ring. (x 3)

The first has been done for you.

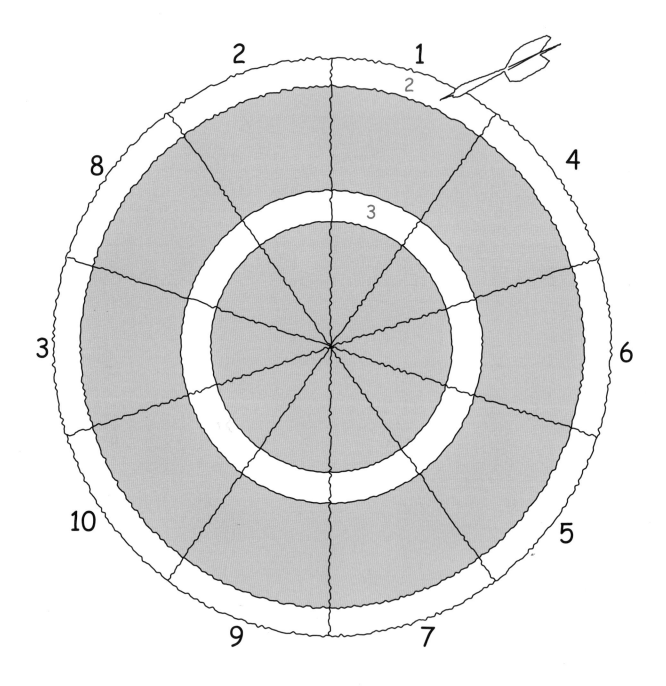

Missing numbers

Fill in the missing numbers.
Use your multiplication square to help you.

---

4 times table

1 $4 \times \underline{\hspace{1cm}} = 8$ **2** $4 \times \underline{\hspace{1cm}} = 40$ **3** $4 \times \underline{\hspace{1cm}} = 12$

4 $4 \times \underline{\hspace{1cm}} = 36$ **5** $4 \times \underline{\hspace{1cm}} = 16$ **6** $4 \times \underline{\hspace{1cm}} = 32$

7 $4 \times \underline{\hspace{1cm}} = 20$ **8** $4 \times \underline{\hspace{1cm}} = 28$ **9** $4 \times \underline{\hspace{1cm}} = 4$

10 $4 \times \underline{\hspace{1cm}} = 24$

---

5 times table

1 $5 \times \underline{\hspace{1cm}} = 10$ **2** $5 \times \underline{\hspace{1cm}} = 40$ **3** $5 \times \underline{\hspace{1cm}} = 25$

4 $5 \times \underline{\hspace{1cm}} = 35$ **5** $5 \times \underline{\hspace{1cm}} = 15$ **6** $5 \times \underline{\hspace{1cm}} = 30$

7 $5 \times \underline{\hspace{1cm}} = 20$ **8** $5 \times \underline{\hspace{1cm}} = 50$ **9** $5 \times \underline{\hspace{1cm}} = 5$

10 $5 \times \underline{\hspace{1cm}} = 45$

Match the sums

Draw a line to match the sums with the answers.
The first has been done for you.

6 times table

| 7 x 6 = | | 10 x 6 = | | 1 x 6 = |

6   24   30

18   54

| 4 x 6 = | 5 x 6 = |

12   36   42

60   48

| 2 x 6 = | 9 x 6 = |

| 3 x 6 = | | 8 x 6 = | | 6 x 6 = |

7 times table

| 7 x 7 = | 7 x 6 = | 7 x 1 = | 7 x 9 = |

14   28

7   42   56

| 7 x 3 = | 7 x 8 = |

21   63

70   35   49

| 7 x 4 = | 7 x 5 = | 7 x 2 = | 7 x 10 = |

Calculations

Match the sums again

Draw a line to match the sums with the answers.
The first has been done for you.

8 times table

| 8 x 1 = | | 8 x 8 = | | 8 x 5 = |

| 8 x 4 = | 32   24   16 | | 8 x 9 = |
| | 40   64 | |

8   48   56

| 8 x 2 = | 80   72 | | 8 x 7 = |

| 8 x 3 = | | 8 x 6 = | | 8 x 10 = |

9 times table

| 7 x 9 = | 6 x 9 = | 1 x 9 = | 9 x 9 = |

27   90

36   54   81

| 3 x 9 = | 18   72 | 8 x 9 = |

63   45   9

| 4 x 9 = | 5 x 9 = | 2 x 9 = | 10 x 9 = |

Multiplication crossnumber

Across

1 3 x 4 = _____

3 9 x 5 = _____

5 7 x 9 = _____

6 4 x 5 = _____

7 3 x 6 = _____

9 10 x 5 = _____

11 4 x 4 = _____

13 6 x 4 = _____

15 7 x 6 = _____

17 7 x 7 = _____

18 5 x 3 = _____

19 5 x 6 = _____

23 6 x 6 = _____

24 2 x 9 = _____

25 5 x 9 = _____

27 8 x 9 = _____

29 3 x 8 = _____

30 9 x 7 = _____

32 8 x 6 = _____

35 3 x 7 = _____

37 4 x 8 = _____

38 9 x 4 = _____

39 9 x 7 = _____

40 8 x 10 = _____

Down

2 7 x 3 = _____

4 9 x 6 = _____

5 8 x 8 = _____

6 5 x 4 = _____

8 9 x 9 = _____

9 6 x 9 = _____

10 4 x 6 = _____

12 8 x 8 = _____

13 5 x 5 = _____

14 5 x 8 = _____

16 9 x 3 = _____

19 7 x 5 = _____

20 10 x 10 = _____

21 8 x 2 = _____

22 3 x 9 = _____

23 5 x 7 = _____

24 7 x 2 = _____

26 7 x 8 = _____

28 8 x 3 = _____

29 7 x 4 = _____

31 8 x 4 = _____

32 6 x 7 = _____

33 8 x 7 = _____

34 4 x 9 = _____

36 6 x 3 = _____

Complete the table of prices.

drinks	cost of 2 bottles	cost of 3 bottles	cost of 4 bottles	cost of 5 bottles	cost of 6 bottles
soft drink £2					
grape juice £3					
cider £4					
wine £5					
sherry £6					
gin £7					
port £8					
whisky £9					
vodka £10					

What is the cost of

1   3 bottles of sherry, 3 bottles of port and 3 bottles of vodka?

_____

2   4 bottles of cider, 4 bottles of sherry and 4 bottles of gin?

_____

3   6 bottles of wine, 5 bottles of whisky and 6 bottles of grape juice?

_____

4   7 bottles of soft drinks, 5 bottles of cider and 3 bottles of vodka?

_____

5   4 bottles of grape juice, 5 bottles of wine and 3 bottles of gin?

_____

Remember

Round 27, 15 and 42 to the nearest 10.

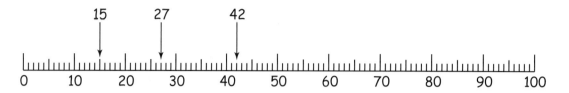

27 is between 20 and 30.
It is **nearer** 30, so it is **rounded up** to **30**.

When the number is half way between, round up.
15 is **half way** between 10 and 20, so 15 is **rounded up** to **20**.

If the number is less than half way round down.
42 is **less than half way** between 40 and 50,
so 42 is **rounded down** to **40**.

Round each number to the nearest 10.

1

number	16	79	22	55	64	38	31	92	25	49
rounded										

2

number	43	29	52	35	17	74	81	69	86	95
rounded										

3 Draw lines to match each item to the rounded price.
The first has been done for you.

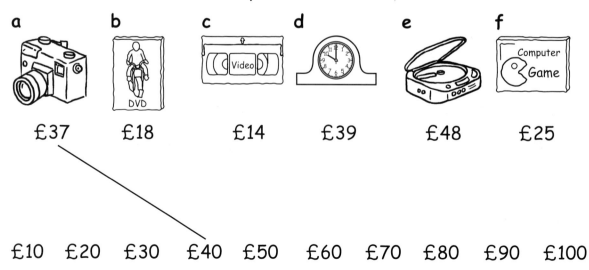

Rounding prices

Round the prices of the tins in each shopping list.

Use the rounded price to estimate the total bill.

1 Tim's shopping list

rounded price _____

_____

total _____

2 Soumia's shopping list

rounded price _____

_____

total _____

3 Judith's shopping list

rounded price _____

_____

total _____

4 Jackie's shopping list

rounded price _____

_____

total _____

5 Yusuf's shopping list

rounded price _____

_____

total _____

6 Jo's shopping list

rounded price _____

_____

total _____

The number of visitors to a kennels is recorded over 5 weekends in the summer.

day	week 1	week 2	week 3	week 4	week 5
Friday	12	15	13	25	21
Saturday	19	24	23	42	26
Sunday	35	41	37	32	44

1 **a** Fill in the table below, rounding the number of visitors to the nearest 10.
   b Use the rounded numbers to estimate the total number of visitors each week.

day	week 1	week 2	week 3	week 4	week 5
Friday					
Saturday					
Sunday					
estimated total					

2 Which day is usually the busiest? _____

3 Which day is always the quietest? _____

4 Which week had the most visitors? _____

5 Which weeks had about the same number of visitors? _____

Match more sums

Draw a line to match the sums.
The first has been done for you.

1 5 and 3 is 8	**a** 6 + 3 = 9
2 6 plus 2 make 8	**b** 5 + 3 = 8
3 6 minus 4 equals 2	**c** 3 + 7 = 10
4 4 and 3 equals 7	**d** 9 – 8 = 1
5 7 take away 2 equals 5	**e** 6 + 2 = 8
6 The sum of 3 and 7 is 10	**f** 7 – 2 = 5
7 6 plus 3 equals 9	**g** 6 – 4 = 2
8 9 subtract 8 is 1	**h** 4 + 3 = 7
9 4 less 1 is 3	**i** 8 – 5 = 3
10 The sum of 3 and 3 is 6	**j** 5 + 4 = 9
11 8 take away 5 is 3	**k** 4 – 1 = 3
12 9 minus 3 equals 6	**l** 3 + 3 = 6
13 5 add 4 is 9	**m** 9 – 3 = 6

Answer each sum.
Draw a line to match the sums.
The first has been done for you.

1 6 – 4 = 2

2 9 – 3 = _____

3 4 + 3 = _____

4 5 plus 5 = _____

5 The total of 4 and 2 is _____

6 8 – 0 = _____

7 4 subtract 3 is _____

8 0 and 8 makes _____

9 9 minus 7 makes _____

10 7 take away 0 equals _____

11 6 + 3 = _____

12 3 + 3 = _____

13 7 add 3 is _____

a _____ = 5 + 5

b _____ = 4 and 2

c _____ = 8 take away 0

d _____ = 9 minus 3

e _____ = 0 + 8

f 2 = 6 subtract 4

g _____ = 4 plus 3

h _____ = 7 + 3

i _____ = the sum of 3 plus 3

j _____ = 6 plus 3

k _____ = 7 less 0

l _____ = 4 – 3

m _____ = 9 – 7

Sums

Answer each sum.

1   10 take away 3 equals _____

2   7 subtract 2 is _____

3   8 minus 6 equals _____

4   8 plus 1 makes _____

5   4 and 5 make _____

6   The total of 3 and 5 is _____

7   8 minus 3 is _____

8   7 add 2 equals _____

9   3 more than 4 is _____

10   The sum of 4 and 6 is _____

11   _____ = 4 and 3

12   _____ = 3 plus 3

13   _____ = 6 take away 2

14   _____ = 5 add 5

15   _____ = 6 subtract 2

16   _____ = 9 minus 3

17   _____ = the sum of 5 and 3

18   _____ = 4 plus 4

19   _____ = 4 more than 5

20   _____ = 6 subtract 5

21   1 and 8 equals _____

22   _____ = the sum of 6 and 2

23   _____ = 5 plus 5

24   7 minus 5 is _____

25   _____ = 5 minus 1

26   6 add 4 = _____

27   The total of 8 and 2 is _____

28   _____ = 5 subtract 3

29   _____ = 2 more than 6

30   9 take away 8 equals _____

Remember

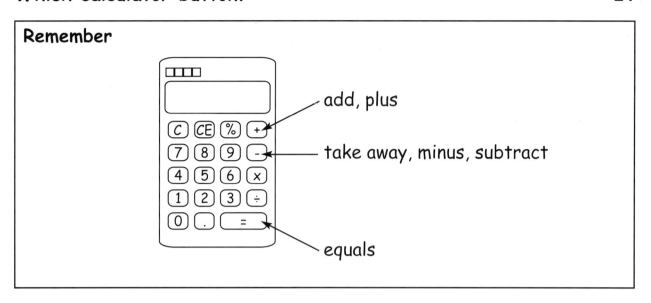

add, plus

take away, minus, subtract

equals

Fill in the buttons you would press to do these sums.
The first one has been done for you.

6 add 3 equals ⬡6 ⬡+ ⬡3 ⬡=

1 6 take away 3 equals

2 6 minus 3 equals

3 6 subtract 3 equals

4 6 plus 3 equals

5 7 plus 2 equals

6 7 take away 1 equals

7 7 minus 2 equals

8 7 add 2 equals

9 5 plus 4 equals

10 5 add 4 equals

11 5 minus 4 equals

12 5 subtract 4 equals

Calculations

Remember

After each sum press Ⓒlear.

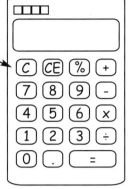

Use a calculator to work these out.

1 4 + 5 =   **2** 3 + 7 =   **3** 8 – 0 =   **4** 5 – 2 =

5 6 – 5 =   **6** 4 – 1 =   **7** 5 + 5 =   **8** 7 + 2 =

9 1 + 8 =   **10** 7 – 3 =   **11** 3 + 3 =   **12** 6 – 0 =

13 4 + 0 =   **14** 0 + 3 =   **15** 5 – 1 =   **16** 8 – 3 =

17 6 plus 4 =   **18** 9 subtract 7 =   **19** 3 add 3 =

20 6 and 3 =   **21** 4 take away 0 =   **22** 8 minus 7 =

23 2 plus 0 =   **24** 5 add 1 =   **25** 4 + 4 =

Use the calculator to check the students' sums.
Mark them with a cross or a tick.
How many have they each got right?

Mohammed	**Steve**	**Jane**
4 + 2 = 6	3 + 2 = 5	7 + 3 = 10
3 – 0 = 2	5 – 0 = 5	5 – 2 = 3
5 + 3 = 8	6 + 3 = 8	4 + 3 = 1
0 + 3 = 3	2 + 3 = 5	5 + 0 = 5
4 – 1 = 5	7 – 1 = 8	4 – 1 = 5
3 + 3 = 6	4 + 4 = 8	6 – 1 = 5
		4 + 3 = 7
total right _____	total right _____	total right _____

Remember

	-	minus, subtract, take away
	+	plus, add, and
	x	times, multiply

Which operation would you use to answer the following questions?
Write the sign in each box.

1 What is the sum of 6 and 7? ☐

2 Take 7 from 15. ☐

3 What are 6 lots of 7? ☐

4 What is 4 more than 13? ☐

5 What is the difference between 8 and 4? ☐

6 What is 4 less than 12? ☐

7 What is the total of 4, 5 and 6? ☐

8 There are 8 cakes in a box. How many cakes in 4 boxes? ☐

Microwave cooking

Write down the cooking time for each item.

Cooking time
in minutes

1 A pizza cooks in 3 minutes. _____

2 Sponge cakes cook for 2 minutes longer than pizza. _____

3 Large potatoes cook for 4 times as long as pizza. _____

4 Curry cooks for twice as long as pizza. _____

5 Rice needs 2 minutes less than curry. _____

6 Chicken cooks for 10 times as long as pizza. _____

7 Christmas cake takes 1 minute longer than sponge cake. _____

8 The cooking time for a piece of chicken is 1 minute
   shorter than the cooking time for rice. _____

9 2 pieces of chicken take 1 minute more than a pizza. _____

10 Beans take 2 minutes less than pizza. _____

+, – and × problems

Work out the answers to the following questions.
Write down your calculations.

1 A paper costs 35p and a bar of chocolate costs 48p.
How much is this altogether?

Answer _____

2 Batteries are sold in packs of 4. How many batteries
are there in 5 packs?

Answer _____

3 A man runs 6 miles each day for 5 days.
How many miles is this altogether?

Answer _____

4 Ben is 46. Jill is 8 years older. How old is Jill?

Answer _____

5 Jack is 57. He will retire at 65.
How many years is it before he retires?

Answer _____

6 A CD player costs £65. Pete has £49.
How much more does Pete need to buy the CD player?

Answer _____

7 A coat costs £56. In a sale it is reduced by £12.
How much is the coat now?

Answer _____

8 Friends drink 14 cans of beer during a football match.
After the match they drink 14 more.
How many cans have they had altogether?

Answer _____

9 8 computer games can be tested in an hour.
How many can be tested in 4 hours?

Answer _____

Calculations

Basketball	£16
Football boots	£45
Shin pads	£9
Shorts	£14
Socks	£4
Tracksuit	£29
Trainers	£26
T-shirt	£10

1 Find the total cost for each person.

Paul		**Jenny**		**Freda**	
shorts	_____	football boots	_____	tracksuit	_____
t-shirt	_____	shin pads	_____	trainers	_____
socks	_____	shorts	_____	2 x socks	_____
total	_____	total	_____	total	_____

2 Debbie has £40. Can she buy a tracksuit and a basketball? _____

3 Ray has £45. Can he buy shorts and trainers? _____

4 Karl has £70. He buys a t-shirt and trainers.
How much does he have left? _____

5 Sandra has £50. She buys shin pads, 2 pairs of socks, a basketball and shorts.
How much does she have now? _____

6 Mohammed wants new football boots. He has £38.
How much more does he need? _____

7 Dev's team need 6 pairs of shin pads. How much will this cost? _____

Coaches come in different sizes.

Coach A   **Coach B**   **Coach C**
Seats 14 people   Seats 32 people   Seats 53 people

What size coaches would you hire for these trips?
You may use more than one coach. Have as few empty seats as possible.

1 29 students on a day trip. _____

2 A netball team with 7 players, 12 supporters and 1 coach. _____

3 A family group of 48 going to a wedding. _____

4 99 football supporters. _____

5 38 people going to the cinema. _____

6 19 adults going bowling with 6 children. _____

7 50 children and 29 adults going to the seaside. _____

8 6 swimming teams each with 4 swimmers and a coach for each team.

_____

9 40 French students and 38 Italian students. _____

10 2 classes of 8 students and 2 teachers for each class. _____

+, - and x with a calculator

Remember

C   clears the entry

CE   clears the last entry you entered

With **subtraction** sums, enter the number you are taking away last.

With addition and multiplication the order does not matter.

Answer these using a calculator.

1   36 + 15 + 21 = _____

2   50 – 26 = _____

3   8 x 0 = _____

4   14 + 29 + 33 = _____

5   54 – 19 = _____

6   8 x 7 = _____

7   44 + 14 + 9 + 6 = _____

8   45 – 26 = _____

9   9 x 9 = _____

10 What is the total of 46, 17 and 6? _____

11 Add together 32 and 41. _____

12 Multiply 6 by 7. _____

13 What is 26 more than 37? _____

14 What is 16 less than 65? _____

15 What is 7 times 5? _____

16 What is 36 minus 9? _____

17 What are 8 lots of 7? _____

Calculations

More calculator problems

1 a A man buys trousers for £34, a shirt for £14 and a tie for £5.
      What is the total cost? _____

   b The man had £60.
      How much will he have left? _____

2 A football match is 90 minutes.
   After 35 minutes a player is sent off.
   How much of the match will he miss? _____

3 a 8 friends each buy 2 burgers.
      How many burgers is this altogether? _____

   b Each burger costs £3.
      What is the total cost? _____

4 Use your calculator to check how many answers each of the students got right.

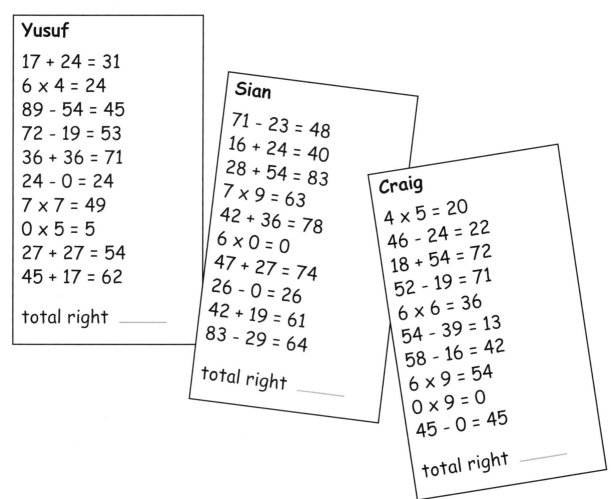

Yusuf

17 + 24 = 31
6 x 4 = 24
89 - 54 = 45
72 - 19 = 53
36 + 36 = 71
24 - 0 = 24
7 x 7 = 49
0 x 5 = 5
27 + 27 = 54
45 + 17 = 62

total right _____

Sian

71 - 23 = 48
16 + 24 = 40
28 + 54 = 83
7 x 9 = 63
42 + 36 = 78
6 x 0 = 0
47 + 27 = 74
26 - 0 = 26
42 + 19 = 61
83 - 29 = 64

total right _____

Craig

4 x 5 = 20
46 - 24 = 22
18 + 54 = 72
52 - 19 = 71
6 x 6 = 36
54 - 39 = 13
58 - 16 = 42
6 x 9 = 54
0 x 9 = 0
45 - 0 = 45

total right _____

Calculations

p21-27

1 Each box needs 10 cans.
   How many cans need to be added to each box?

a  needs ____ cans.   b  needs ____ cans.

c needs ____ cans.   d needs ____ cans.

p55-57

2 A box has 10 bottles. Jenny takes 3 bottles.
   Tick the sums that find the number of bottles left.

   3 + 10 =   10 – 3 =   3 – 10 =

   ten take away three =   three plus ten =

p21-27

3 A pack has 8 cans. Jill takes 4.
   How many are left? _____

p55-57

4 Max has 4 bottles. Mohammed has 5 bottles.
   Tick the sums that find the total number of bottles.

   5 – 4 =   5 + 4 =   4 + 5 =

   five add four =   5 take away 4 =

p21-27

5 Jag has 3 cans. Pete has 7 cans.
   How many cans are there altogether? _____

6 Sam has 9 cans. Paul has 2 less than Sam.
   How many cans has Paul got? _____

Calculations

Skill check

Skill check

```
                      Student café

coffee        50p         cake              42p
tea           48p         biscuit           27p
soft drink    46p         cereal bar        35p
fruit juice   34p         chocolate bar     43p
```

p28-41

1 Fiaz has a cup of coffee and a biscuit.

   a How much is this? _____

   b How much change will she have from 80p? _____

2 Rhonda has a cup of tea and a cereal bar.

   a How much is this? _____

   b How much change will she have from 90p? _____

3 What is the difference in price between fruit juice and soft drinks?

   _____

4 Jenny has a cake and a chocolate bar.
   Tick the sum that finds the cost.

      43p – 42p =   42p + 43p =   42 x 43p =

5 There are 45 biscuits in a box.
   38 biscuits are sold.
   How many biscuits are left in the box? _____

Meals	
burger	£2
pizza	£3
curry	£4

p42-51

6 Pete buys 3 pizzas. Tick the sums that find the cost of the pizzas.

3 x 3 x 3 =   3 + 3 + 3 =   3 x 3 =

7 Tim has £10. He buys 2 curries.

a How much is this? _____

b How much change will he have? _____

8 Yui has £20. She buys 4 burgers and 2 pizzas.

a How much is this? _____

b How much change will she have? _____

9 The café orders 3 boxes of pizzas. There are 5 pizzas in each box.

How many pizzas is this? _____

p60

10 Tick the words that mean the same as X

times   add   multiply   subtract   lots of

p52-54

11 Round the prices on the menu to the nearest 10p.

			rounded to the nearest 10p
a	tea	48p	_____
b	soft drink	46p	_____
c	fruit juice	34p	_____
d	cake	42p	_____
e	cereal bar	35p	_____
f	biscuits	27p	_____
g	chocolate bar	43p	_____

Calculations skill check 1 answers

1 a 4

   b 7

   c 6

   d 8

2 10 − 3 =   ten take away three =

3 4

4 5 + 4 =   4 + 5 =   five add four =

5 10

6 7

Calculations skill check 2 answers

1 a 77p   b 3p
2 a 83p   b 7p

3 12p

4 42p + 43p =

5 7

6 3 x 3 =   3 + 3 + 3 =

7 a £8   b £2

8 a £14   b £6

9 15

10 times   multiply   lots of

11 a 50p   b 50p

    c 30p   d 40p

    e 40p   f 30p

    g 40p

> **Remember**
>
> half = $\frac{1}{2}$
>
> $\frac{1}{2}$  $\frac{1}{2}$
>
> The 2 on the bottom shows the whole thing has been cut into 2 pieces.
>
> Each piece must be the same size.

1 Tick the objects that have been cut in half.

cake

apple

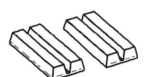

chocolate bar

pie

sausage

orange

bread

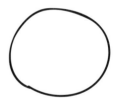

pizza

banana

sausage roll

naan bread

2 Tick the containers that are $\frac{1}{2}$ full.

ink cartridge

beer

bottle

coke

Remember

quarter = $\frac{1}{4}$

The 4 on the bottom shows the whole thing has been cut into 4 pieces.

Each piece must be the same size.

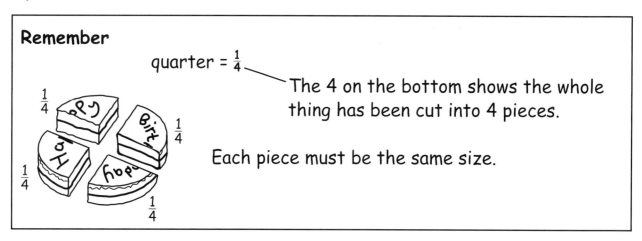

1 Tick the objects that have been cut in quarters.

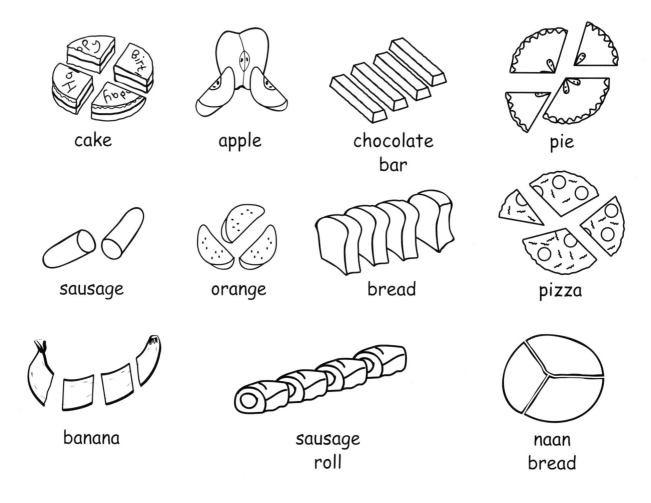

cake	apple	chocolate bar	pie
sausage	orange	bread	pizza
banana		sausage roll	naan bread

2 Tick the containers that are $\frac{1}{4}$ full.

ink cartridge	beer	bottle	coke

$\frac{1}{2}$ or $\frac{1}{4}$

Name each fraction $\frac{1}{2}$ or $\frac{1}{4}$.

The first has been done for you.

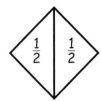 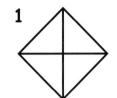 1 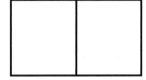 2  3

4 Draw lines to cut the shapes below in half.

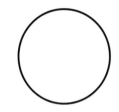  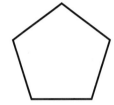 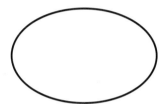

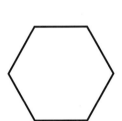  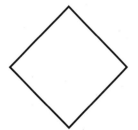 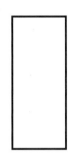

5 Draw lines to cut the shapes below into quarters.

 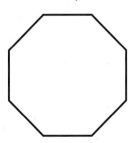  

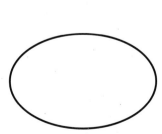 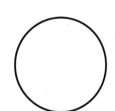 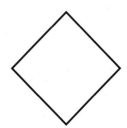

What fraction?

How much is shaded?

 1 of the 2 pieces is shaded.
$\frac{1}{2}$

 3 of the 4 pieces are shaded.
$\frac{3}{4}$

What fraction of these shapes is shaded?

1 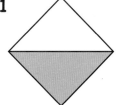 2 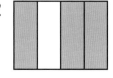 3 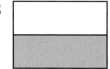 4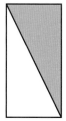

5 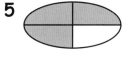 6 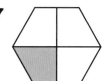 7   8

9  10 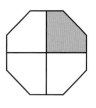 11 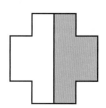 12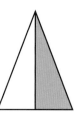

13 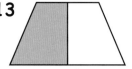 14 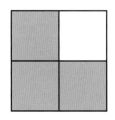 15 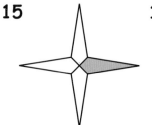 16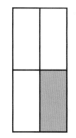

Fractions

How much chocolate?

1 chocolate bar is cut in half.   1 chocolate bar is cut in quarters.

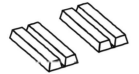   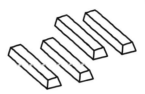

Draw lines to match the same amount of chocolate.
Write the amount on the line.

1 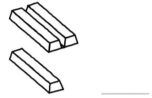 _____

a   _____

2  _____

b 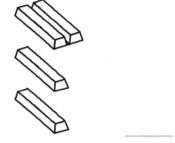 _____

3  _____

c 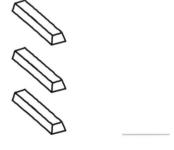 _____

4 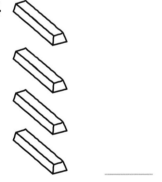 _____

d  _____

5 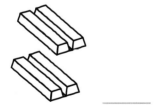 _____

e 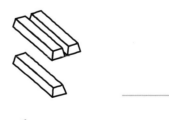 _____

6 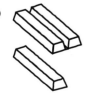 _____

f   _____

How much is left?

What fraction of the chocolate bar is left in each case?

1

Karl eats $\dfrac{1}{2}$ Fraction left: _____

2

Paul eats $\dfrac{1}{4}$ Fraction left: _____

3

Yui eats $\dfrac{1}{4}$ and Ray eats $\dfrac{1}{2}$ Fraction left: _____

4

Jane eats $\dfrac{1}{4}$, Rhonda eats $\dfrac{1}{4}$ and Soumia eats $\dfrac{1}{4}$ Fraction left: _____

5

Marie eats $\dfrac{1}{4}$ and Debbie eats $\dfrac{1}{4}$ Fraction left: _____

6

Kim eats $\dfrac{1}{4}$, Tom eats $\dfrac{1}{2}$ and Maroof eats $\dfrac{1}{4}$ Fraction left: _____

$\frac{1}{2}$ of the packet

Draw a circle round half of the contents in each packet.
Write the number of items in each half.

1

6 cheeses

$\frac{1}{2}$ of 6 cheeses = _____ cheeses

2

8 cheese strips

$\frac{1}{2}$ of 8 cheese strips = _____ cheese strips

3

10 pepperoni sticks

$\frac{1}{2}$ of 10 pepperoni sticks = _____ pepperoni sticks

4

4 burgers

$\frac{1}{2}$ of 4 burgers = _____ burgers

5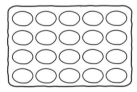

20 nuggets

$\frac{1}{2}$ of 20 nuggets = _____ nuggets

6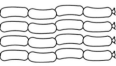

16 sausages

$\frac{1}{2}$ of 16 sausages = _____ sausages

7

18 chocolates

$\frac{1}{2}$ of 18 chocolates = _____ chocolates

$\dfrac{1}{4}$ **of the packet**

Draw a circle round quarter of the contents in each packet.
Write the number of items in each quarter.

1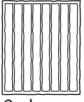

8 cheese strips

$\frac{1}{4}$ of 8 cheese strips = _____ cheese strips

2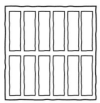

12 fish fingers

$\frac{1}{4}$ of 12 fish fingers = _____ fish fingers

3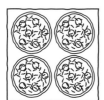

4 pizzas

$\frac{1}{4}$ of 4 pizzas = _____ pizza

4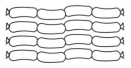

16 sausages

$\frac{1}{4}$ of 16 sausages = _____ sausages

5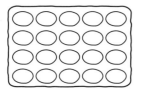

20 nuggets

$\frac{1}{4}$ of 20 nuggets = _____ nuggets

6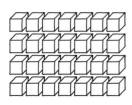

28 stock cubes

$\frac{1}{4}$ of 28 stock cubes = _____ stock cubes

7

24 pegs

$\frac{1}{4}$ of 24 pegs = _____ pegs

Fractions

> **Remember**
>
>   To find $\frac{1}{2}$ the whole is cut into 2 equal amounts
>
>   To find $\frac{1}{4}$ the whole is cut into 4 equal amounts

Find half of each amount.

1 $\frac{1}{2}$ of 6 = _____

2 $\frac{1}{2}$ of 10 = _____

3 $\frac{1}{2}$ of 26 = _____

tablets

4 $\frac{1}{2}$ of 14 = _____

5 $\frac{1}{2}$ of 2 = _____

6 $\frac{1}{2}$ of 18 = _____

Find half and quarter of each amount.

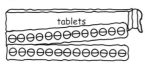 **7** **a** $\frac{1}{2}$ of 8 = _____

   b $\frac{1}{4}$ of 8 = _____

 **8** **a** $\frac{1}{2}$ of 12 = _____

   b $\frac{1}{4}$ of 12 = _____

 9 **a** $\frac{1}{2}$ of 20 = _____

   b $\frac{1}{4}$ of 20 = _____

 **10** **a** $\frac{1}{2}$ of 16 = _____

   b $\frac{1}{4}$ of 16 = _____

 **11** **a** $\frac{1}{2}$ of 4 = _____

   b $\frac{1}{4}$ of 4 = _____

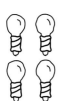

 **12** **a** $\frac{1}{2}$ of 24 = _____

   b $\frac{1}{4}$ of 24 = _____

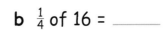

To find a quarter, $\frac{1}{2}$ and $\frac{1}{2}$ again.

Example   What is $\frac{1}{4}$ of 20?

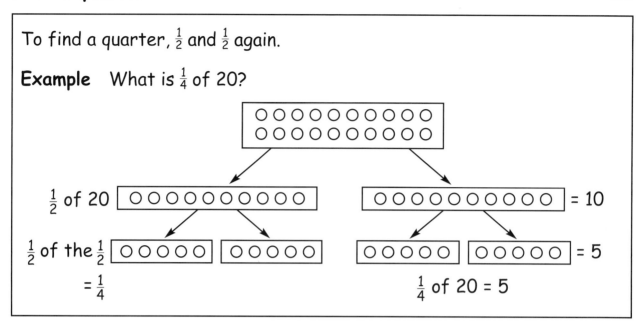

Find $\frac{1}{2}$ and then $\frac{1}{4}$ of each of these amounts.

	$\frac{1}{2}$	$\frac{1}{4}$
4		
12		
8		
20		
60		
16		
40		
24		
80		

Fractions

Half your money

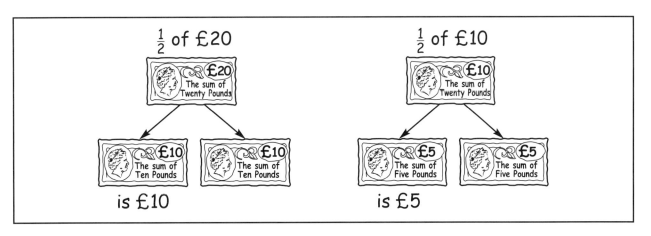

$\frac{1}{2}$ of £20 ... is £10

$\frac{1}{2}$ of £10 ... is £5

What is $\frac{1}{2}$ of these amounts of money?

1 £60 _____ **2** £80 _____ **3** £100 _____ **4** £30 _____

5 £70 _____ **6** £50 _____ **7** £90 _____ **8** £40 _____

These items are $\frac{1}{2}$ price.

Write the sale price on the ticket.

9 Was £60 Now _____

10 Was £70 Now _____

11 Was £20 Now _____

12 Was £50 Now _____

13 Was £30 Now _____

14 Was £40 Now _____

Fractions

Fractions puzzle

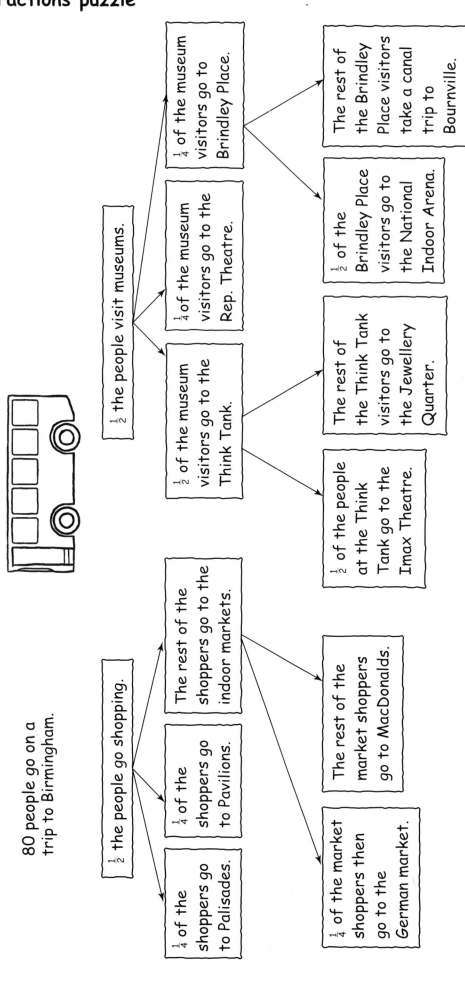

80 people go on a trip to Birmingham.

$\frac{1}{2}$ the people go shopping.

$\frac{1}{4}$ of the shoppers go to Palisades.

$\frac{1}{4}$ of the shoppers go to Pavilions.

The rest of the shoppers go to the indoor markets.

$\frac{1}{4}$ of the market shoppers then go to the German market.

The rest of the market shoppers go to MacDonalds.

$\frac{1}{2}$ the people visit museums.

$\frac{1}{4}$ of the museum visitors go to Brindley Place.

$\frac{1}{4}$ of the museum visitors go to the Rep. Theatre.

$\frac{1}{2}$ of the museum visitors go to the Think Tank.

The rest of the Brindley Place visitors take a canal trip to Bournville.

$\frac{1}{2}$ of the Brindley Place visitors go to the National Indoor Arena.

The rest of the Think Tank visitors go to the Jewellery Quarter.

$\frac{1}{2}$ of the people at the Think Tank go to the Imax Theatre.

How many people does the coach driver need to pick up from each of these places?

1 National Indoor Arena _____   **2** Pavilions _____   **3** Imax Theatre _____   **4** MacDonalds _____   **5** Bournville _____

6 Palisades _____   **7** Jewellery Quarter _____   **8** German market _____   **9** Rep. Theatre _____

Fraction problems

1 Ben is half his sister's age. His sister is 14 years old. How old is Ben?

2 Jag is going on holiday. She drives for 40 miles and stops for a break. If she is half way now, how far is the full journey?

3 Tom buys a coat for £40. He has spent $\frac{1}{2}$ his money. How much did he have to start with?

4 Jim walks each day for 40 minutes. His friend walks with him for $\frac{1}{4}$ of the time. How long is this each day?

5 Max wins £28. He spends $\frac{1}{4}$ on lottery tickets.
   a How much does he have left?
   b What fraction is this?

6 A CD is £15 in a $\frac{1}{2}$ price sale. What was its normal selling price?

7 There are 20 chocolates in a box. Jenny eats $\frac{1}{4}$ of the box. How many chocolates are left?

8 The dinner has to cook for 30 minutes. It needs to be stirred $\frac{1}{2}$ way through. After how many minutes is this?

9 There are 16 people waiting to see the nurse or doctor. $\frac{1}{4}$ of the people want to see the nurse. How many people want to see the doctor?

10 Debbie spends $\frac{1}{4}$ of her money on a book. The book costs £6. How much money did Debbie have to start with?

11 Tim has £18. He spends $\frac{1}{2}$ of it on food. How much has he spent?

12 Joe is $\frac{1}{4}$ of his sister's age. Joe is 5 years old. How old is his sister?

Fractions skill check

a   b   c   d

1 a Tom orders $\frac{1}{2}$ pizza. Which is Tom's pizza? _____

   b Sam has $\frac{1}{4}$ pizza. Which is Sam's pizza? _____

a   b   c

2 a Tom has drunk $\frac{1}{2}$ of the bottle. Which is Tom's bottle? _____

   b Yusuf has drunk $\frac{1}{4}$ of his bottle. Which is Yusuf's bottle? _____

p77-79

3 a Sarah eats half of her pizza.
How many pieces is this? _____

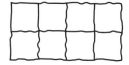

   b Zoe eats $\frac{1}{4}$ of her pizza.
How many pieces is this? _____

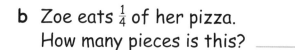

4 a $\frac{1}{4}$ of this family pizza is pepperoni.
How many pieces is this? _____

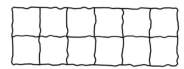

   b $\frac{1}{2}$ of the family pizza is cheese
and tomato.
How many pieces is this? _____

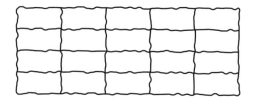

5 $\frac{3}{4}$ of this family pizza is Hawaiian.
How many pieces is this? _____

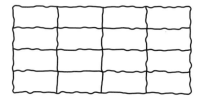

6 The sauce bottle is $\frac{1}{4}$ full.
Colour the bottle to show $\frac{1}{4}$ full.

7 The vinegar bottle is $\frac{1}{2}$ full.
Colour the bottle to show $\frac{1}{2}$ full.

8 Draw lines to cut these pizzas in half.
Show 4 different ways to cut the pizzas.

9 Satvinder has a pizza. He eats $\frac{1}{2}$ of it. How much is left? _____

10 Paul has a pizza. He eats $\frac{1}{4}$ of it. How much is left? _____

11 Jag has a pizza. She eats $\frac{3}{4}$ of it. How much is left? _____

12 Karl is half his sister's age. His sister is 12. How old is Karl? _____

13 Cilla spends half of her money on a new coat. The coat cost £20.
How much money did Cilla have to start with? _____

Fractions

Fractions skill check answers

1 a b
  b d

2 a c
  b b

3 a 4
  b 3

4 a 5
  b 10

5 12

6

7

8

9 $\frac{1}{2}$

10 $\frac{3}{4}$

11 $\frac{1}{4}$

12 6

13 £40

1 How many footballs are there? _____

2 a How many rugby balls are there? _____

  b How many more rugby balls are there than footballs? _____

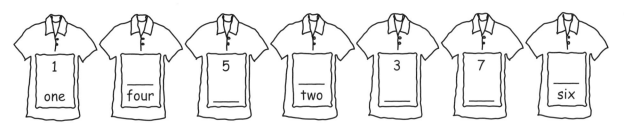

3 a How many t-shirts are there? _____

  b Write the missing numbers on the t-shirts.

  c Write the t-shirt numbers in order.
     The first 2 have been done for you.

     1   2   _____   _____   _____   _____   _____

Afternoon matches
Football   1:00–3:00
Rugby   2:00–4:00
Cricket   3:00–5:00

4 a Which is the first match? _____

  b Which is the 3rd match? _____

Mock Test

5 Draw a line to match the cups with the badges.

Football results

Chasers 4 goals : Kickers 6 goals

---

6 How many goals altogether? _____

7 Which team had the most goals? _____

8 Add these points to the points table:

   a add 2 points to Kickers

   b add 1 point to Strikers

   c add 1 point to Targets

Points table

Kickers	6	_____
Strikers	3	_____
Targets	4	_____

---

9 Use the answers from question 8.
The Chasers have 10 points.
How many more points do the other teams need to have 10 points?

   a Kickers need _____ points

   b Strikers need _____ points

   c Targets need _____ points

10 There are ten bottles in a box.
Karl takes 2 bottles.
Tick the sums that find the number of bottles left in the box.

   10 – 2   two take away ten   ten take away two

   10 subtract 2   two plus ten   10 + 2

11 a There are ten cans in a box. Max takes 2 cans.

     How many cans are left? _____

   b Then Ben takes 3 cans.

     How many cans are left now? _____

12 Ray puts 4 cans in the bin. Mick puts 3 cans in the bin.

   How many cans are in the bin? _____

13 Draw a line to match the sums.

   3 + 5 =   5 + 4 =

   4 + 5 =   5 + 2 =

   2 + 5 =   5 + 3 =

Mock Test

| bananas | oranges | pineapple | oranges | bananas | pineapples |

1 How many are there of each item:

   a bananas _____   **b** oranges _____   **c** pineapples _____

2 Round each of the following to the nearest 10.

   a 32 _____   **b** 19 _____   **c** 35 _____

3 Bags have 10 apples.

   a Tara buys 4 bags of apples.
   How many apples is this? _____

   b Tim buys 6 bags of apples.
   How many apples is this? _____

4 Bags have 2 lemons.

   a Jill buys 4 bags of lemons.
   How many lemons is this? _____

   b Yui buys 6 bags of lemons.
   How many lemons is this? _____

5 Nerys eats 2 bananas each day for a week. How many bananas is this?

6 Fill in the missing numbers.

| 5 | 10 | | 20 | 25 | | 35 | | 45 | |

Mock Test

7 a Bananas cost 56p.
Write this number in words. _____

b Pineapples cost seventy five pence.
Write this in numbers. _____

8 a Find the cost of these shopping lists:

Sally		Mohammed		Steve	
bananas	36p	pears	14p	pineapples	75p
apples	34p	lemons	18p	oranges	12p
total	____	total	____	total	____

b Sally pays with 80p. How much change will she have? _____

c Mohammed pays with 50p. How much change will he have? _____

d Steve pays with 90p. How much change will he have? _____

9 Boxes have 60 apples.
24 apples have been sold. How many apples are left? _____

10 The shop keeper has 4 boxes of bananas.
Each box hold 30 bananas.
Tick the sums that give the total number of bananas.

30 – 4   30 + 4   30 + 30 + 30 + 30   30 x 4

11 The shop keeper has sold 46 boxes of fruit.
He started with 85 boxes.
Tick the sum that gives the number of boxes left.

46 + 85   85 – 46   8 x 46

12 Max eats half of his apple. How much is left? _____

13 Jim eats $\frac{1}{4}$ of a box of strawberries. How much is left? _____

14 Jenny drinks half of her carton of orange juice.
Which carton is half full? _____

a   b   c   d

15 Which box of oranges is $\frac{1}{4}$ full? _____

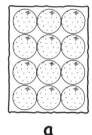 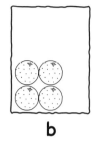 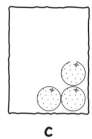 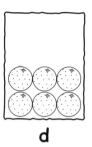

a   b   c   d

16 A box holds 22 oranges.
$\frac{1}{2}$ of the oranges are sold. How many are left? _____

17 A box has 20 bananas. $\frac{1}{4}$ have gone bad. How many is this? _____

18 A box holds 24 pineapples. $\frac{1}{4}$ are sold. How many are left? _____

19 At the end of the day, bags of fruit are sold at half price.
What is the sale price of these bags?

a   b   c

 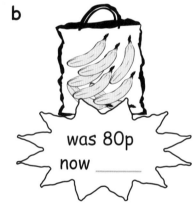 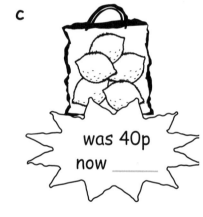

was 60p   was 80p   was 40p

now _____   now _____   now _____

20 The fruit baskets are marked $\frac{1}{4}$ off.
What is the new price for the baskets?

a   b   c

was £8   was £12   was £4

now _____   now _____   now _____

Mock Test

Numbers

Count to 10 and back
1 6
2 7
3 10
4 6
5 1
6 4
7 2, 4, 7, 9
8 8, 4, 2

How many tins?
1 four 4
2 nine 9
3 seven 7
4 one 1
5 three 3
6 eight 8
7 five 5
8 six 6
9 two 2
10 ten 10

Count to 10
1 seven 7
2 one 1
3 four 4
4 three 3
5 eight 8
6 nine 9
7 three 3
8 five 5
9 six 6
10 zero 0

Numbers in words and figures
1 a 1   b 10
   c 5   d 8
   e 6   f 3
2 a two   b six
   c eight d ten
   e three f seven
3 a 2   b 4
   c 7   d 9
   e 8   f 3
4 a four   b one
   c five   d nine
   e three f seven

Which floor?
1 2   2 6
3 4   4 3
5 8   6 9
7 5   8 1
9 10

Bus stop
1 Tim
2 Pete
3 Ben
4 Jo
5 Raj
6 Jill
7 Pete
8 Max
9 6th
10 5th
11 8th
12 3rd

More or less?
1 a less b more
2 a more b less
3 a more b less
4 a more b less
5 a more b less

Count and count on
1 a 2   b 4
2 a 4   b 6
3 a 6   b 9
4 a 5   b 9
5 a 3   b 6
6 a 2   b 3
7 a 6   b 10
8 a 5   b 9
9 a 7   b 9
10 a 3   b 5
11 a 8   b 10

Count to 20
1 16   2 12
3 20   4 18
5 14   6 19
7 12   8 18
9 14   10 15

Count in 2s
1 2, 4, 6, 8, 10, 12, 14, 16, 18
2 12
3 26
4 34
5 18
6 22
7 16

Count in 10s
1 30
2 42
3 67
4 86
5 45

Count on in 10s
1 a 18   b 22
   c 19   d 26
   e 32   f 41
   g 34   h 46
   i 24   j 55
   k 63   l 37
2 a 16   b 23
   c 17   d 25
   e 52   f 67
   g 81   h 75
3 a 42p
   b 54p
   c 68p
   d 82p
   e 76p
   f 58p
   g 71p
   h 24p

Tens and units

		T	U
1	3 Tens 6 Units	3	6
2	2 Tens 7 Units	2	7
3	6 Tens 1 Unit	6	1
4	7 Tens 3 Units	7	3
5	4 Tens 0 Units	4	0
6	4 Tens 8 Units	4	8
7	5 Tens 0 Units	5	0
8	1 Ten 3 Units	1	3
9	0 Tens 7 Units	0	7
10	8 Tens 0 Units	8	0
11	0 Tens 3 Units	0	3
12	1 Ten 6 Units	1	6

Having a test
1 8 pens, 10 pencils, 12 rulers, 10 erasers
2 20 pens, 20 pencils, 24 rulers, 20 erasers
3 50 pens, 40 pencils, 50 rulers, 40 erasers
4 50 pens, 60 pencils, 50 rulers, 60 erasers
5 100 pens, 80 pencils, 100 rulers, 80 erasers

Odd and even numbers
1 6, 14, 20, 26, 32, 42
2 Ask your maths tutor to check this for you
3 7, 11, 19, 27, 31
4 Ask your maths tutor to check this for you
5 odd 31, 25, 39
   even 6, 14

Odd one out
1 a yes b no c yes
2 a yes b no c yes
3 a yes b no c no
4 a yes b no c yes

Answers

Calculations

Page 21

Add up the bottles
1 7
2 5
3 9
4 10
5 9
6 9
7 7
8 9
9 8
10 10

Page 22

Make ten
1 9
2 4
3 8
4 3
5 2
6 6
7 5
8 7
9 1

Page 23

Make ten again
1 0→10 1→9 2→8
   3→7 4→6 5→5
   6→4 7→3 8→2
   9→1 10→0
2 a 6
   b 5
   c 3
   d 8
   e 1
3 zero→ten
   one→nine
   two→eight
   three→seven
   four→six
   five→five

Page 24

How many more?
1 3
2 5
3 5
4 1
5 2
6 2
7 7

Page 25

Make connections
1 a 2   b 4

8	–	2	=	6
–		+		+
6	–	4	=	2
=		=		=
2	+	6	=	8

2 a 3   b 1

7	–	4	=	3
–		–		+
3	+	1	=	4
=		=		=
4	+	3	=	7

3 a 7   b 5

9	–	7	=	2
–		–		+
2	+	5	=	7
=		=		=
7	+	2	=	9

4 a 3   b 3

8	–	3	=	5
–		–		+
3	+	0	=	3
=		=		=
5	+	3	=	8

5 a 4   b 4

10	–	4	=	6
–		+		+
6	–	2	=	4
=		=		=
4	+	6	=	10

Page 26

Shopping
1 a £5   b £8
   c £10   d £10
2 a £2   b £2
   c £2   d £7
3 a £8   b £4
   c £1   d £0
   e £7   f £9
   g £2   h £3
   i £5   j £6

Page 27

College classes
1 8
2 6
3 8
4 6
5 6
6 10
7 1
8 2
9 4
10 2
11 2
12 3

Page 28

Add up in your head
1 23
2 37
3 41
4 54
5 61
6 76
7 81
8 94

Page 29

Add in columns
1 58   2 69
3 99   4 78
5 77   6 88
7 81   8 81
9 64   10 80
11 75   12 92
13 83   14 70
15 88   16 64
17 91   18 68
19 80   20 82
21 70   22 67
23 87   24 56

Page 30

One way to add up in your head
1 51   2 58
3 57   4 59
5 72   6 81
7 71

Page 31

Other ways to add up in your head
1 73
2 55
3 85
4 63
5 80
6 91
7 71
8 81
9 90
10 63
11 91
12 82
13 91
14 90
15 73
16 72
17 79
18 80

Page 32

Addition problems
1 51 years old
2 34 people
3 24 cards
4 £55
5 31 cars
6 38 years old
7 22nd September
8 £33
9 £53
10 35 people

Page 33

Prizes
Ask your maths tutor to check this for you

Page 34

Matches

1 41		**2** 59	
3 63		**4** 93	
5 84		**6** 96	
7 91		**8** 53	
9 61		**10** 85	
11 64		**12** 45	

Page 35

Make connections again

1 a 3   **b** 0

16	–	3	=	13
–		+		+
3	–	0	=	3
=		=		=
13	+	3	=	16

2 a 15   **b** 11

19	–	15	=	4
–		–		+
4	+	11	=	15
=		=		=
15	+	4	=	19

3 a 12   **b** 7

17	–	12	=	5
–		–		+
5	+	7	=	12
=		=		=
12	+	5	=	17

4 a 8   **b** 1

15	–	8	=	7
–		–		+
7	+	1	=	8
=		=		=
8	+	7	=	15

5 a 6   **b** 0

18	–	6	=	12
–		–		+
6	+	0	=	6
=		=		=
12	+	6	=	18

Page 36

Subtract in your head

1 9
2 11
3 13
4 9
5 15
6 7
7 9

Page 37

Other ways to subtract in your head

1 24
2 17
3 27
4 20
5 30
6 20
7 27
8 27
9 36
10 31
11 38
12 47
13 39
14 25
15 59
16 37
17 29
18 64

Page 38

Subtract in columns

1 20
2 16
3 17
4 41
5 52
6 32
7 13
8 45
9 17
10 44
11 36
12 71

Page 39

Subtraction practice

1 56		**2** 23		**3** 32	
4 28		**5** 29		**6** 74	
7 28		**8** 48		**9** 36	
10 35		**11** 5		**12** 18	

Ellie	Jake	Yusuf	Rajaa
£11	£28	£36	£52
£32	£49	£57	£73
£26	£43	£51	£67
£23	£40	£48	£64
£38	£55	£63	£79
£12	£29	£37	£53

Page 40

Subtraction problems

1 23 TVs
2 12 days
3 £26
4 15 people
5 35 treats
6 11 tickets
7 £14
8 9 patients
9 8 tins
10 65 minutes

Page 41

Attendance

1 14		**2** 7	
3 36		**4** 21	
5 19		**6** 8	
7 11		**8** 29	
9 31			

Page 42

Multiplication

1 30		**2** £10	
3 24		**4** 40	
5 18			

Page 43

Match them up

1 8 c
2 32 a
3 18 b
4 21 e
5 16 g
6 27 d
7 42 i
8 20 f
9 28 h

Page 44

Another odd one out

1 3 x 3
2 2 x 8
3 7 x 3
4 4 x 8
5 6 x 2
6 3 x 3
7 7 x 3
8 4 x 7
9 5 x 7

Page 45

Table sequences

2s: 2, 4, 6, 8, 10, 12, 14, 16, 18, 20

3s: 3, 6, 9, 12, 15, 18, 21, 24, 27, 30

4s: 4, 8, 12, 16, 20, 24, 28, 32, 36, 40

5s: 5, 10, 15, 20, 25, 30, 35, 40, 45, 50

6s: 6, 12, 18, 24, 30, 36, 42, 48, 54, 60

7s: 7, 14, 21, 28, 35, 42, 49, 56, 63, 70

8s: 8, 16, 24, 32, 40, 48, 56, 64, 72, 80

9s: 9, 18, 27, 36, 45, 54, 63, 72, 81, 90

10s: 10, 20, 30, 40, 50, 60, 70, 80, 90, 100

Page 46

Mini darts

score 1 double 2, triple 3

score 2 double 4, triple 6

score 3 double 6, triple 9

score 4 double 8, triple 12

score 5 double 10, triple 15

score 6 double 12, triple 18

score 7 double 14, triple 21

score 8 double 16, triple 24,

score 9 double 18, triple 27

score 10 double 20, triple 30

Page 47

Missing numbers

4x

1	2
2	10
3	3
4	9
5	4
6	8
7	5
8	7
9	1
10	6

5x

1	2
2	8
3	5
4	7
5	3
6	6
7	4
8	10
9	1
10	9

Page 48

Match the sums

$1 \times 6 = 6$

$2 \times 6 = 12$

$3 \times 6 = 18$

$4 \times 6 = 24$

$5 \times 6 = 30$

$6 \times 6 = 36$

$7 \times 6 = 42$

$8 \times 6 = 48$

$9 \times 6 = 54$

$10 \times 6 = 60$

$7 \times 1 = 7$

$7 \times 2 = 14$

$7 \times 3 = 21$

$7 \times 4 = 28$

$7 \times 5 = 35$

$7 \times 6 = 42$

$7 \times 7 = 49$

$7 \times 8 = 56$

$7 \times 9 = 63$

$7 \times 10 = 70$

Page 49

Match the sums again

$8 \times 1 = 8$

$8 \times 2 = 16$

$8 \times 3 = 24$

$8 \times 4 = 32$

$8 \times 5 = 40$

$8 \times 6 = 48$

$8 \times 7 = 56$

$8 \times 8 = 64$

$8 \times 9 = 72$

$8 \times 10 = 80$

$1 \times 9 = 9$

$2 \times 9 = 18$

$3 \times 9 = 27$

$4 \times 9 = 36$

$5 \times 9 = 45$

$6 \times 9 = 54$

$7 \times 9 = 63$

$8 \times 9 = 72$

$9 \times 9 = 81$

$10 \times 9 = 90$

Page 50

Multiplication crossnumber

¹1	²2		³4	⁴5		⁵6	3		⁶2	0
	⁷1	⁸8		4		4		⁹5	0	
¹⁰2		¹¹1	¹²6				¹³2	4		¹⁴4
¹⁵4	¹⁶2		¹⁷4	9		¹⁸1	5		¹⁹3	0
	7				²⁰1				5	
					0					
	²¹1				0			²²2		
²³3	6		²⁴1	8		²⁵4	²⁶5		²⁷7	²⁸2
5		²⁹2	4				³⁰6	³¹3		4
	³²4	8		³³5		³⁴3		³⁵2	³⁶1	
³⁷3	2		³⁸3	6		³⁹6	3		⁴⁰8	0

Page 51

Bottle sales

drinks	cost of 2 bottles	cost of 3 bottles	cost of 4 bottles	cost of 5 bottles	cost of 6 bottles
soft drink £2	£4	£6	£8	£10	£12
grape juice £3	£6	£9	£12	£15	£18
cider £4	£8	£12	£16	£20	£24
wine £5	£10	£15	£20	£25	£30
sherry £6	£12	£18	£24	£30	£36
gin £7	£14	£21	£28	£35	£42
port £8	£16	£24	£32	£40	£48
whisky £9	£18	£27	£36	£45	£54
vodka £10	£20	£30	£40	£50	£60

1 £18 + £24 + £30 = £72
2 £16 + £24 + £28 = £68
3 £30 + £45 + £18 = £93
4 £14 + £20 + £30 = £64
5 £12 + £25 + £21 = £58

Page 52

Round to the nearest 10
1 20, 80, 20, 60, 60, 40, 30, 90, 30, 50
2 40, 30, 50, 40, 20, 70, 80, 70, 90, 100
3 a £40   b £20
   c £10   d £40
   e £50   f £30

Page 53

Rounding prices
1 30p + 60p = 90p
2 40p + 50p = 90p
3 50p + 40p = 90p
4 20p + 60p = 80p
5 50p + 50p = £1
6 20p + 60p = 80p

Page 54

Kennel visitors

day	week 1	week 2	week 3	week 4	week 5
Friday	10	20	10	30	20
Saturday	20	20	20	40	30
Sunday	40	40	40	30	40
estimated total	70	80	70	100	90

2 Sunday
3 Friday
4 week 4
5 week 1 and week 3

Page 55

Match more sums
1 b   2 e
3 g   4 h
5 f   6 c
7 a   8 d
9 k   10 l
11 i   12 m
13 j

Page 56

Now match these
1 2 f   2 6 d
3 7 g   4 10 a
5 6 b   6 8 c
7 1 l   8 8 e
9 2 m   10 7 k
11 9 j   12 6 i
13 10 h

Page 57

Sums
1 7
2 5
3 2
4 9
5 9
6 8
7 5
8 9
9 7
10 10
11 7
12 6
13 4
14 10
15 4
16 6
17 8
18 8
19 9
20 1
21 9
22 8
23 10
24 2
25 4
26 10
27 10
28 2
29 8
30 1

Page 58

Which calculator button?
1 6 − 3 =
2 6 − 3 =
3 6 − 3 =
4 6 + 3 =
5 7 + 2 =
6 7 − 1 =
7 7 − 2 =
8 7 + 2 =
9 5 + 4 =
10 5 + 4 =
11 5 − 4 =
12 5 − 4 =

Page 59

Use a calculator
1. 9
2. 10
3. 8
4. 3
5. 1
6. 3
7. 10
8. 9
9. 9
10. 4
11. 6
12. 6
13. 4
14. 3
15. 4
16. 5
17. 10
18. 2
19. 6
20. 9
21. 4
22. 1
23. 2
24. 6
25. 8

Mohammed
4 + 2 = 6 ✓
3 − 0 = 2 ✗
5 + 3 = 8 ✓
0 + 3 = 3 ✓
4 − 1 = 5 ✗
3 + 3 = 6 ✓
total right 4

Steve
3 + 2 = 5 ✓
5 − 0 = 5 ✓
6 + 3 = 8 ✗
2 + 3 = 5 ✓
7 − 1 = 8 ✗
4 + 4 = 8 ✓
total right 4

Jane
7 + 3 = 10 ✓
5 − 2 = 3 ✓
4 + 3 = 1 ✗
5 + 0 = 5 ✓
4 − 1 = 5 ✗
6 − 1 = 5 ✓
4 + 3 = 7 ✓
total right 5

Page 60

Operations − + x
1. +
2. −
3. ×
4. +
5. −
6. −
7. +
8. ×

Page 61

Microwave cooking
1. 3
2. 3 + 2 = 5
3. 4 × 3 = 12
4. 2 × 3 = 6
5. 6 − 2 = 4
6. 10 × 3 = 30
7. 5 + 1 = 6
8. 4 − 1 = 3
9. 3 + 1 = 4
10. 3 − 2 = 1

Page 62

+, − and x problems
1. 83p
2. 20 batteries
3. 30 miles
4. 54 years old
5. 8 years
6. £16
7. £44
8. 28 cans
9. 32 games

Page 63

Sports equipment
1. Paul £14 + £10 + £4 = £28
   Jenny £45 + £9 + £14 = £68
   Freda £29 + £26 + £4 + £4 = £63
2. no
3. yes
4. £34
5. £3
6. £7
7. £54

Page 64

Hiring a coach
1. B
2. AA
3. C
4. CBA
5. AAA
6. AA
7. CAA
8. B
9. BBA
10. AA

Page 65

+, − and x with a calculator
1. 72
2. 24
3. 0
4. 76
5. 35
6. 56
7. 73
8. 19
9. 81
10. 69
11. 73
12. 42
13. 63
14. 49
15. 35
16. 27
17. 56

Page 66

More calculator problems
1. a £53
   b £7
2. 55 minutes
3. a 16 burgers
   b £48

Yusuf
17 + 24 = 31 ✗
6 × 4 = 24 ✓
89 − 54 = 45 ✗
72 − 19 = 53 ✓
36 + 36 = 71 ✗
24 − 0 = 24 ✓
7 × 7 = 49 ✓
0 × 5 = 5 ✗
27 + 27 = 54 ✓
45 + 17 = 62 ✓
total right 6

Sian
71 − 23 = 48 ✓
16 + 24 = 40 ✓
28 + 54 = 83 ✗
7 × 9 = 63 ✓
42 + 36 = 78 ✓
6 × 0 = 0 ✓
47 + 27 = 74 ✓
26 − 0 = 26 ✓
42 + 19 = 61 ✓
83 − 29 = 64 ✗
total right 8

Craig
4 × 5 = 20 ✓
46 − 24 = 22 ✓
18 + 54 = 72 ✓
52 − 19 = 71 ✗
6 × 6 = 36 ✓
54 − 39 = 13 ✗
58 − 16 = 42 ✓
6 × 9 = 54 ✓
0 × 9 = 0 ✓
45 − 0 = 45 ✓
total right 8

Answers

Fractions

Halves

1 objects ticked are cake, chocolate bar, pie, bread, pizza, banana
2 objects ticked are beer, coke

Quarters

1 objects ticked are cake, chocolate bar, bread, banana, sausage roll
2 objects ticked are ink cartridge, coke

$\frac{1}{2}$ or $\frac{1}{4}$

1

2

$\frac{1}{2}$	$\frac{1}{2}$

3

$\frac{1}{4}$	$\frac{1}{4}$	$\frac{1}{4}$	$\frac{1}{4}$

4 These are some possible answers. Ask your maths tutor to check any other answers you have.

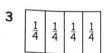

5 These are some possible answers. Ask your maths tutor to check any other answers you have.

What fraction?

1 $\frac{1}{2}$ 2 $\frac{3}{4}$
3 $\frac{1}{2}$ 4 $\frac{1}{2}$
5 $\frac{3}{4}$ 6 $\frac{1}{2}$
7 $\frac{1}{4}$ 8 $\frac{1}{2}$
9 $\frac{1}{2}$ 10 $\frac{1}{4}$
11 $\frac{1}{2}$ 12 $\frac{1}{2}$
13 $\frac{1}{2}$ 14 $\frac{3}{4}$
15 $\frac{1}{4}$ 16 $\frac{1}{4}$

How much chocolate?

1 c or e = $\frac{3}{4}$
2 a or f = $\frac{2}{4}$ or $\frac{1}{2}$
3 a or f = $\frac{2}{4}$ or $\frac{1}{2}$
4 b or d = 1 whole
5 b or d = 1 whole
6 c or e = $\frac{3}{4}$

How much is left?

1 $\frac{1}{2}$ 2 $\frac{3}{4}$
3 $\frac{1}{4}$ 4 $\frac{1}{4}$
5 $\frac{1}{2}$ 6 none

$\frac{1}{2}$ **of the packet**

1 3
2 4
3 5
4 2
5 10
6 8
7 9

$\frac{1}{4}$ **of the packet**

1 2   2 3
3 1   4 4
5 5   6 7
7 6

Find half and quarter

1 3
2 5
3 13
4 7
5 1
6 9
7 a 4   b 2
8 a 6   b 3
9 a 10   b 5
10 a 8   b 4
11 a 2   b 1
12 a 12   b 6

Find a quarter

	$\frac{1}{2}$	$\frac{1}{4}$
4	2	1
12	6	3
8	4	2
20	10	5
60	30	15
16	8	4
40	20	10
24	12	6
80	40	20

Half your money

1 £30   2 £40
3 £50   4 £15
5 £35   6 £25
7 £45   8 £20
9 £30   10 £35
11 £10   12 £25
13 £15   14 £20

Fractions puzzle

1 5   2 10
3 10   4 15
5 5   6 10
7 10   8 5
9 10

Fraction problems

1 7 years old
2 80 miles
3 £80
4 10 minutes
5 a £21
   b $\frac{3}{4}$
6 £30
7 15 chocolates
8 15 minutes
9 12 people
10 £24
11 £9
12 20 years old

Number mock tests

Number mock test 1

1 5

2 a 7   b 2

3 a 7

   b

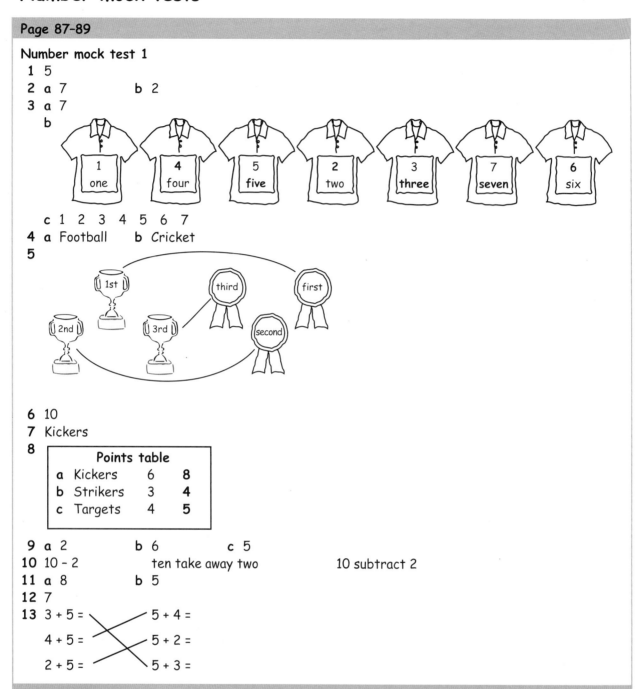

   c 1 2 3 4 5 6 7

4 a Football   b Cricket

5

6 10

7 Kickers

8

Points table		
a Kickers	6	**8**
b Strikers	3	**4**
c Targets	4	**5**

9 a 2   b 6   c 5

10 10 – 2   ten take away two   10 subtract 2

11 a 8   b 5

12 7

13 3 + 5 =   5 + 4 =

    4 + 5 =   5 + 2 =

    2 + 5 =   5 + 3 =

Number mock test 2

1 a 15   b 14   c 13   **2** a 30   b 20   c 40

3 a 40   b 60   **4** a 8   b 12

5 14   **6** 15   30   40   50   **7** a fifty-six   b 75p

8 a Sally 70p   Mohammed 32p   Steve 87p

   b 10p   c 18p   d 3p

9 36

10 30 + 30 + 30 + 30 =   30 x 4 =

11 85 – 46 =   **12** $\frac{1}{2}$ **13** $\frac{3}{4}$

14 c   **15** c   **16** 11

17 5   **18** 18

19 a 30p   b 40p   c 20p   **20** a £6   b £9   c £3

BTEC NATIONAL
FOR IT PRACTITIONERS

CORE

MARK FISHPOOL
BERNADETTE FISHPOOL

HODDER
EDUCATION

PART OF HACHETTE LIVRE UK

Acknowledgements

For Dorothy, Mary and John – with love.

Our thanks to Christopher Ashwood for all photographic content in Unit 29 and Josie Ashwood for photographic content in Unit 1.

Every effort has been made to contact copyright holders and the publishers will be glad to make suitable arrangements with any copyright holders that it has not been possible to contact.
The authors and publishers would like to thank the following for the use of images in this volume. Screenshots of Microsoft products and applications are copyright of Microsoft corporation.

1.14 – ©iStockphoto.com/Steve Luker; **1.15** – © Shannon Mendes / Masterfile; **2.1** – ©iStockphoto.com/Dino Ablakovic; **2.2 and 2.21** – © CoverSpot / Alamy; **2.25** © Jonas Engström / iStockphoto.com; **2.27** © Christian Dones / iStockphoto.com; **2.29** © Norman Chan / iStockphoto.com; **2.49** – lewing@isc.tamu.edu/ The GIMP; **2.66** – ©iStockphoto.com/Andrew Howe; **3.16a and 3.16b** – Mower Magic Ltd; **8.21** – Lloyds TSB; **8.25** – Wikipedia – http://www.wikipedia.org; **8.27** – ©iStockphoto.com/ Shaun Lowe; **15.2** – APACS; **15.3** – Ebay.co.uk; **15.5** – ©iStockphoto.com/ pmphoto , Peter Mautsch, Dortmund, Germany; **15.8** –BSA – Business software alliance; **15.9** – FAST; **15.10** – BCS – British Computing Society; **15.11** – ACM - Advancing Computing as a Science & Profession; **22.15** – Mutiny Ltd; **27.3** – C?!? Systems; **29.1** – ©2006 interface.centraltreasure.com; **29.3** – © copyright 2001–2007 The Sims Zone; **29.10** – Test Tools Europe Limited; **29.11** – © istockphoto.com / Dainis Derics; **29.27** – Google Inc.; **29.34** – www.hse.gov.uk/electricity - Reproduced under the terms of the Click-Use License; **29.35** – Electrical Safety Council; **29.39** – http://www.firekills.gov.uk/electrical/02.htm/ – Reproduced under the terms of the Click-Use License; **29.41** – http://www.hse.gov.uk/firstaid/legislation.htm – Reproduced under the terms of the Click-Use License; **34.2** – PriceRunner.co.uk; **34.3** – Royal Mail; **34.4** – Nokia; **34.07** – © HMV 2007; **34.12** – Everyclick.com; **34.16, 34.17, 34.18, 34.19, 34.20, 34.24 and 34.25** – Google Inc.; **34.27** – www.pcworld.co.uk – © DSG Retail LTD 2007; **34.29** – GoodSearch – www.goodsearch.com; **34.30** – www.charitycafe.com; **34.32** – www.charitycafe.com; **34.33** – www.virginmedia.com; **34.34** – Amazon.co.uk; **35.2** – © Roger Ressmeyer/CORBIS; **35.5** – © Chad Ehlers / Alamy; **35.11** – © Dennis MacDonald / Alamy; **35.16** – UPS.

Orders: please contact Bookpoint Ltd, 130 Milton Park, Abingdon, Oxon OX14 4SB. Telephone: (44) 01235 827720. Fax: (44) 01235 400454. Lines are open from 9.00–5.00, Monday to Saturday, with a 24 hour message answering service. You can also order through our website www.hoddereducation.co.uk

If you have any comments to make about this, or any of our other titles, please send them to
educationenquiries@hodder.co.uk

British Library Cataloguing in Publication Data
A catalogue record for this title is available from the British Library

ISBN: 978 0 340 941 812

This Edition Published 2007
Impression number   10 9 8 7 6 5 4 3 2
Year   2012, 2011, 2010, 2009 2008

Hachette Livre's policy is to use papers that are natural, renewable and recyclable products and made from wood grown in sustainable forests.The logging and manufacturing processes are expected to conform to the environmental regulations of the country of origin.

Cover photo from © Larry Williams/Corbis.
Typeset by Pantek Arts Ltd, Maidstone, Kent.
Printed in Italy for Hodder Education, an Hachette Livre UK Company, 338 Euston Road, London NW1 3BH.